Anonymous

Keeping one Cow

Being the Experience of a number of practical Writers, in a clear and condensed Form, upon the Management of a single Milch Cow

Anonymous

Keeping one Cow
Being the Experience of a number of practical Writers, in a clear and condensed Form, upon the Management of a single Milch Cow

ISBN/EAN: 9783337176884

Printed in Europe, USA, Canada, Australia, Japan

Cover: Foto ©ninafisch / pixelio.de

More available books at **www.hansebooks.com**

KEEPING ONE COW.

BEING THE EXPERIENCE OF A NUMBER OF PRACTICAL WRITERS,
IN A CLEAR AND CONDENSED FORM,

UPON THE

MANAGEMENT OF A SINGLE MILCH COW.

ILLUSTRATED.

NEW YORK:
ORANGE JUDD COMPANY,
751 BROADWAY.
1884.

TABLE OF CONTENTS.

Absorbents in the Stable.....14, 17, 19, 26, 53, 75, 80, 94, 99, 127
Accounts, Dr. and Cr.....11, 21, 38, 45, 111, 113, 131
Ailments.................28, 89, 115
Alfalfa Clover...................97
" " Cut six times.........98
Artichokes, Jerusalem..........64-77
" Feeding...........69, 75
" Nutritive Value of...75, 76
Barley as an Autumn Crop.........107
Barn—See Stable..................
Barre System of Feeding............105
Butter........................14
Buying Feed..................78, 93
Brewer's Grains............9, 109, 130
Calf, Care and Disposal of the...12, 21, 27, 28, 57, 62, 71, 89, 119
" Rations for..............21, 28
" Scours in.................28
" Teaching to Drink......12, 22, 28
Clover, White and Red, compared..104
Corn (Indian) for Fodder..12, 17, 20, 25, 29, 31, 44, 60
Compost Heap..................19, 81
Cow, Care at Calving Time...21, 27, 41, 50, 72, 83, 87, 114
" Carding..............37, 56, 84
" Drying Off.........14, 37, 87
" Fat at Calving..........110, 114
" General Treatment...9, 17, 30, 37, 50, 96, 98, 119
" How to Select a.............80
" Kept in the North..........9
" Kept in New York.....78, 99, 123
" Kept in the South..........25
" Kept in the Eastern States...35, 92, 103, 110
" Kept in the Town........108, 130
" Kept in Ohio..............53
" Kept in Pennsylvania......16, 64
" Kept in Indiana............119
" Kept on Cape Cod............92
" Kept in California..........97
" Kept in Connecticut.......110
" Points of a Good............9
" Rations for........29, 30, 37, 43
" Stabled in Town............108
" Yield of Milk.15, 42, 57, 72, 114, 132
Cow Doctors....................89
Diseases—See Ailments...........
Draining Land..................125
Drouth, Effects of, on Milk........39
Dry Fodder for Winter......87, 108
Dung Heap, the................125
Ellsworth's, System of Feeding....105
Exercise, Need of............81, 109
Fastening for the Stable.........63
Feeding, System of...18, 27, 29, 37, 43, 83, 105
Fertilizers, Commercial.47, 59, 117, 118
Food, Am't Required for a Year.10, 64
" " " Daily......106
Garget (Inflamed Udder)......89, 115
Grasses, Mixed, as Soiling Crops..103
Grass Seed Mixtures.............103
Ground Feed, Bran.........37, 87
" " Cotton-seed Oil Cake Meal......29, 44, 87
" " Corn Meal....37, 57, 59

Ground Feed, Oats and Peas........10
Hay.................30, 82, 100
Hay Tea........................28
Hungarian Grass................108
Land, Area Required....9, 11, 16, 22, 47, 64-65, 78, 82, 93, 99, 106, 117-118, 125
Land, None Absolutely Required...130
" Sloping to the South and East.125
Leaves as Bedding.............18, 94
Litter for Bedding.........18, 55, 80
Manure...................11, 100, 125
" Care of....19, 26, 62, 74, 80, 126
" Liquid....................128
" Supply Increased by Soiling. 88
Milk Flavored by Turnips..........14
" " Weeds.........103
" In the Family. 11, 14, 58, 90, 130
Milking..................13, 62, 83
" Three Times a Day.72, 102, 104
" Prior to Calving....27, 41, 115
Milk-Pail......................50
Muck, Value as an Absorbent.....80
Parturition..............50, 72, 87
Pasturing..................39, 82
Peas, Canada Field.............92
" Cow......................30
Pea-Vine Hay..................30
Pearl Millet.........21, 31, 116
Pigs to Work Over Manure....94, 127
" to Consume Sour Milk..58, 79, 90
Profits of Keeping One Cow..11, 35, 45, 58, 90, 115, 130
Rotation..................65-66, 83, 91
Roots, Culture of.......19, 41, 98, 107
" Cutting Up...............18
" Storing in Pits.12, 20, 37, 95, 108
" Storing in Barrels..........95
Root Crops, Artichokes......64, 70, 75
" " Carrots.........20, 43
" " Mangels..........12
" " Parsnips..........87
" " Sugar-Beets......16, 19, 60
" " Turnips.........42, 93
Root Cellar...................128
Salting........................122
Sea-Weed as an Absorbent........94
Shade in the Yard..............81
Soiling Crops.............21, 25, 92
" " Alfalfa...............97
" " Artichokes...........64
" " Cabbages......32, 94
" " Canada Peas........92
" " Cow Peas...........30
" " Golden Millet....25, 31
" " Hungarian Grass..92, 108
" " Minnesota Corn......92
" " Mixed Grasses......103
" " Oats and Peas......92
" " Peas...............11
" " Rye...........20, 108
Stables, Plans, etc...10, 17, 25, 48, 49, 72-73, 78-79, 94, 121, 126-127-128
Stable Requisites............11, 63
Stable-Tie....................63
Tethering................116, 119
Tank for Liquid Manure........128
Udder, Inflammation of......89, 115
Vermin........................36
Water............10, 26, 44, 84, 103
Weeds Flavoring Milk..........103

(v)

PUBLISHERS' ANNOUNCEMENT.

We have now, according to the last census, a population pressing close upon fifty Millions. Every one of this vast number is individually interested in the milk question. What is true of perhaps no other element of food and nourishment, milk is consumed in some form by all, old and young. It is because of this necessarily universal personal interest in milk that the publishers offer this volume which aims to show all how to obtain the best milk, plenty of it, and at the cheapest rates. The book embraces the experience and advice of able, well known writers—such, for example, as Professor Slade, of Harvard College, and Henry E. Alvord—elicited in response to propositions presented by the Publishers for articles upon the subject. The editorial supervision of the work has been in the hands of Col. Mason C. Weld and Professor Manly Miles—recognized authorities on Dairy Matters—who would have included many other valuable and interesting papers submitted, were it not that they would have made the volume too bulky. Mr. Orange Judd has added a leaf from his personal experience.

The topics treated are only those legitimately connected with the subject, yet they cover a wide field, and will prove of great interest to all occupied in the culture of the soil, while as a handbook and guide to those who keep one or more family cows it must be of almost daily practical use. The prominent subjects, such as soiling, stabling, care of manure, the tillage of the soil, the cultivation of various crops, care of the cow and of the calf, are each treated in detail, and yet there is so great a variety and such genuine personal experience and sincere conviction on the part of each writer, that his or her way is the best way—as indeed it may be, under the circumstances—that there is little or nothing of sameness or repetition in the book, but the reader's interest is sustained to the last.

INTRODUCTION.

Every farmer is ordinarily supposed to keep several cows, and there is no reason why most families in villages and very many in cities should not possess at least one. Good milk affords the best of nourishment for young children, and goes a long way in saving butchers' bills, and in the preparation of palatable nourishing food of many varieties. Two to five families, according to age and number, can readily unite in having one cow kept, dividing the milk and expenses, and thus always have good, pure, rich milk at very moderate cost. The suitable refuse from the kitchens of three or four families would very much reduce the cost of purchased food. In rural villages, summer pasturage can be obtained near at hand, which, with a daily feed of good meal will furnish a large supply of rich milk at a low cost. A boy can be secured at a small price to drive the cow to the pasture in the morning, and return her at night to the stable. A stable or stall can always be obtained at a trifling rent, and be kept clean. There are plenty of gardeners or farmers who will gladly take the manure away so frequently as to prevent it being a nuisance, or disagreeable.

We have no doubt that all residents of villages, manufacturing towns, etc., can, by arrangements like the above, secure an abundant supply of pure, rich, fresh, healthful milk at less than three cents per quart, and at the same time add greatly to their home comforts, and preserve the health if not the lives of their little ones.

In February, 1880, the publishers of this volume offered prizes for three essays on keeping one cow, indicating at the same time their scope. Some extracts from the explanatory remarks accompanying this offer may fitly outline an introduction to the work.

The number of persons who possess but one cow is far larger than those who have ten or more. No doubt many others, living outside of closely built cities, would gladly lessen the cost of supporting their families, and at the same time add to their comforts, and even luxuries, by keeping a cow, did they know how to keep one. There is a general notion that keeping a cow requires a pasture. If a pasture is not necessary, they do not know how to get along without one. Dairymen and farmers learn how to treat herds as a part of general farm management, or in books on the subject. There are books on cows, but none on one cow. It is not a question of dairy farming, but of dairy gardening. The offer was made to elicit information to enable one to keep a single cow with the best possible results. The main points to be considered are: the stabling or housing of the cow; the yard room she requires, and the storage or disposal of her manure; the least area of land that can be safely set apart for the support of the cow, and how can that land be best managed. It is to be assumed that the land will be made to produce all that it will profitably yield, which will bring up the question of manure and fertilizers, of course considering that produced by the cow herself. What proportion of the produce of the land is to be cured for winter? How much food must be bought, and what? How is the cow to be fed, and in every respect how treated so as to give the best returns to her owner? What should be done at calving time and afterwards? milking, etc. In short, the problem is—given a good cow, how to get the best possible returns from the least possible portion of the land through the agency of the cow.

This, we think, is satisfactorily answered, if not by any one writer, certainly by several combined.

We place as a frontispiece the portrait of a most famous and excellent cow—not so much for her beauty or on account of her breed, but as a model of a dairy cow, and one which may be carried in the mind when purchasing.

KEEPING ONE COW.

THE FAMILY COW AT THE NORTH.

BY MRS. G. BOURINOT, OTTAWA, CANADA.

She's broad in her hips and long in her rump,
A straight and flat back without ever a hump,
She's wide in her lips and calm in her eyes,
She's fine in her shoulders and thin in her thighs,
She's s'eight in her neck and small in her tail,
She's wide in her breast and good at the pail ;
She's fine in her bone and silky of skin,
She's a grazier without and a butcher within.
—MILBURN.

There are several ways of providing for the wants of a cow, but in all cases it is absolutely necessary, in order to obtain the best results, that certain rules be followed with regard to the treatment the cow receives. She must be fed and milked at regular times be kept thoroughly clean, have plenty of fresh air and water, and her food composed of those substances that will keep her always in good condition, do away with the milk bill, reduce the grocer's account, and contribute greatly to the health and comfort of the family. I have tried various things, and have found fresh grass or fodder, provender, bran, oil-cake, mangels, and hay, the best bill of fare for "Daisy" or "Buttercup." Avoid brewer's slops or grains as you would poison, for although they increase the flow of milk, it is thin and blue, the butter white and tasteless, and after a time the cow's teeth will blacken and decay. I was told the other day by a very intelligent dairyman that after feeding his cows one season on brewer's grains he was obliged to sell his whole herd.

YARD, STABLE, AND RATIONS.

Mr. Geo. E. Waring, Jr., in his "Ogden Farm Papers," says he expects to be able to feed a cow from May fifteenth to November fifteenth from half an acre of ground, but the average citizen had better not attempt it, but keep his half acre to raise vegetables and fruit, buying the food required to keep his cow. A cow can be made very profitable if kept in the following way; First, as to the accommodation required, a yard fifteen feet by fifteen, and a stable or cow-shed arranged as in the following plan. *A*, manure shed; *B*, bin for dried earth; *C*, cow; *D*, store-room; *E*, window for putting in hay; *F*, door; *G*, trap to loft; *H*, feeding trough. Have her food provided as follows: into a common pail put one quart

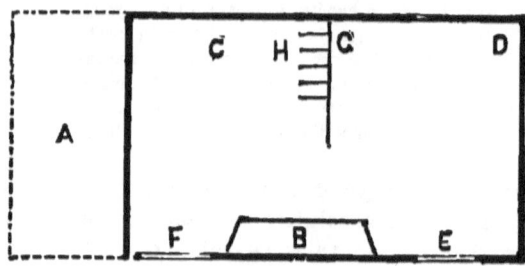

Fig. 1.—STABLE AND YARD.

of provender ("provender" is oats and peas ground together, and can be purchased at any feed store), one-quarter pound of oil-cake, then fill the pail nearly full of bran and pour boiling water over the whole; stir well with a stick, and put it away covered with an old bit of carpet until feeding time; give her that mess twice a day. Have her dinner from June to November consist of grass or fodder cut and brought in twice a week by some farmer or market gardener in exchange for her manure and sour milk. In Montreal, grass and fodder are brought to market by the "Habatants," and sold in bundles. As to quantity, a good big armful will be sufficient, and it is more healthful for the cow if it is a little wilted. In the winter hay and mangels are to be fed in place of the grass and fodder. She should also have salt where she can take a lick when so minded, and fresh water three times a day. The yard should be kept clean by scraping up the manure every morning into the little shed at the end of the stable.

The following table shows the food required to keep one cow through the entire year:

Hay, the best, two tons, at $10 per ton	$20.00
200 pounds of Oil-cake, at $4 per 100 pounds	8.00
800 pounds of Provender, at $1 per 100 pounds	8.00
Half a ton of Bran, at $12 per ton	6.00
One ton of Mangels	5.00
	$47.00

KEEPING ONE COW.

Your cow will require the following "trousseau":

One five-gallon stone churn	$1.25
One and a half dozen milk pans, at $2	3.00
One milk pail and strainer	.60
One butter bowl (wooden)	.50
One paddle and print	.20
Two wooden pails for feed	.40
One card	.25
	$ 6.20
Cost of a good cow	40.00
Interest at 6 per cent	$ 3.69

Any ordinary family will take from a milkman at least one quart a day. We in Ottawa pay eight cents per quart, making per year (365 × 8,) $29.20.

It is a very poor cow that will not average five pounds of butter a week for forty weeks, and that at twenty-five cents per pound, that is 40 (weeks) × 5 (pounds), × 25 (cents), equals 50 (dollars).

So the account stands thus:

Butter	$50.00
Milk	29.20
	$79.20
Cost of food for one year $47.00 ⎱	50.69
Interest on cow and trousseau 3.69 ⎰	
Profit	$28.51

LAND AND CROPS.

I have found that two acres of land is the least possible area that will provide cow-food for the entire year, and that should be divided thus: One acre for hay, the other for fodder and mangels. If you have no land already seeded down, plow up your acre, sow clover and timothy, six pounds, of each. In May, when the grass has fairly started, top-dress it with two bushels of land plaster; if you can apply it just before a rain it is the best time. The first year you will have all clover hay, and it must be cut before the second blossom comes; if not cut early enough, the stalks become tough and woody, and are wasted by the cow. The second year, if top-dressed in the fall with the manure collected during the summer, you will have a fine crop of timothy, and if the land was good for anything you can cut hay from it for three years by giving it a little manure every fall. As early as the ground will admit, sow some peas and oats; one bushel of each will plant one-third of an acre. Peas do well on old sod, and are the best crop to plant on new ground. In about six weeks you can commence cutting it for fodder, and it should give the cow two good meals a day until corn comes in. L. B. Arnold, in "American Dairying," says of corn: "When too thickly planted its stems and leaves are soft and pale, its juices thin and poor. If sown thin or in drills, so that the air and light and heat of the sun can reach it, and not fed until nearly its full size, it is a valuable soiling plant." Now Mr. Waring, in "Farming for Profit," says: "It is a common mistake when the corn is planted in drills to put in so little seed that the stalks grow large and strong, when they are neglected by the cattle, the leaves only being consumed. There should be forty grains at least to the foot of row, which will take from four to six bushels to the acre, but the result will fully justify the outlay, as the corn standing so close in the row will grow fine and thick." My experience tells me that Mr. Waring is right; any way, my cow will not eat the coarse stalks which will grow when the corn is planted too thin.

The one-third acre reserved for mangels, must be the perfection of richness, well drained, and manured. If the soil is deep, you can plant them on the flat, but if the soil is shallow, plant them on ridges, the ridges thirty inches apart (I always plant them in that way); then thin out the plants to fifteen inches apart. Ten to twelve hundred bushels may be grown on an acre, but the ground must be properly prepared. In storing them, they require to be very carefully handled, as the least bruise hastens decay, and we want to keep them fresh and good until April, when our cow ought to give us a calf.

WEANING THE CALF.

I thought I had tried almost everything relating to the care of cows, but when I undertook to wean a five-weeks'-old calf, I found my education in that respect sadly neglected. I asked a farmer's wife how I was to manage. "Oh," she said, "just dip your fingers in the milk, and let the calf suck them a few times, and it will soon learn to put its nose in the pail and drink." It sounded simple enough, so I took my pail and started for the barn, where that wretched animal slopped me all over with milk, bunted me round and round the pen, until I was black and blue, sucked the skin off my finger, and wouldn't drink. After trying at intervals for two days, the calf was getting thin, and so was I. In despair, I left the pail of milk, giving that calf a few words of wholesome advice. When I went back two hours after, the calf was standing over the empty pail, with an expression on its face, that I translated into an inquiry, as to why I hadn't left that pail there before.

I have weaned several calves since then, but have never had any trouble. Leave them with the cow three or four days, then take a little milk and hold the calf's nose in the pail; it must open its mouth or smother, and when once it tastes the milk will soon learn to drink.* When it is a week old, commence feeding with oil-cake, skim-milk and molasses. Into an old two-pound peach can, I put one tablespoonful of oil-cake and one of molasses, fill up the can with boiling water, and set it on the stove until thoroughly cooked. That quantity will be its allowance for one day, mixed with skim-milk. The next week give it that quantity at each meal, and the next week twice that. The calf will then be four weeks old, and the butcher ought to give you a price for it that will pay for all trouble and the family milk bill while the cow was dry. It does not pay to raise calves where you only keep one cow. (Mr. Cochrane, the owner of the celebrated cow " Duchess of Airdrie," told me the other morning that last year he sold a calf of her's to an English gentleman for four thousand guineas (twenty thousand dollars). I think it would pay to have a wet nurse if one had a calf like that). A tablespoonful of lime-water put in the milk now and then will prevent the calf from " scouring," a complaint very common among calves brought up by hand. I believe that winter rye makes a valuable soiling plant, but I have never tried it.

A FEW WORDS AS TO GENERAL MANAGEMENT.

I think it cruel to keep cows tied up all summer. They do not require much exercise, but fresh air they must have, and it is a great comfort to them to lick themselves, although they ought to be well curried every day. It is better to milk after feeding, as they stand more quietly. Don't allow your milk-maid to wash the cow's teats in the milk pail, a filthy habit much in vogue. Insist on her taking a wet cloth and wiping the cow's bag thoroughly before she commences to milk. A cow ought to be milked in ten minutes, although the first time I undertook to milk alone, I tugged away for an hour. I knew how much milk I ought to have, and I was bound to get it. An old cow will eat more than a young one, but will give richer milk. If you can get a cow with her second calf, you can keep her profitably for five years, when she should be sold to the butcher. There is nothing that

---

* It is better, as a rule, not to allow the calf to suck at all. Aptness in learning to drink is influenced by heredity. Calves from ancestors that have not been allowed to suck, learn to drink more readily than those which have been allowed to run with the dam.

will keep your cow-shed so neat, and add so much to the value of your manure pile, as a few shovelfuls of dry earth or muck thrown under the cow. It will absorb the liquid manure better than anything else. Don't allow your milk pans to be appropriated for all sorts of household uses; you cannot make sweet, firm butter if the milk is put into rusty old tin. Skim the milk twice a day into the stone churn; add a little salt, and stir it well every time you put in fresh cream. Use spring water, but don't allow ice to come in contact with the butter; it destroys both color and flavor. If your cream is too warm the butter will come more quickly, but it will be white and soft. When the cream is so cold that it takes me half an hour to churn, I always have the best butter. Don't put your hands to it, work out the buttermilk with a wooden paddle, and work in the salt with the same thing. There is an old saying that one quart of milk a day gives one pound of butter a week, and I think it a pretty fair rule, but don't expect to buy a cow that will give you thirty quarts of milk a day. There are such cows I know, but they are not for sale. Be quite satisfied if your cow gives half that quantity. Place the cow's food where she cannot step on it, but don't put it high up; it is natural for them to eat with their heads down. I think it is better that the family cow should have a calf every year, provided you can have them come early in the spring or late in the autumn. As to the time that a cow should be dry, that depends much upon the way the cow was brought up. If she was allowed to go dry early in the season with her first calf, she will always do it. A cow being a very conservative animal, she should be milked as long as her milk is good. When she is dry stop feeding the provender, bran, and oil-cake, and give her plenty of good hay, with some roots, until after she calves. The provender and oil-cake being strong food, are apt to produce inflammation and other troubles at calving time. You can feed turnips when she is dry, at the rate of two pails a day, cut up fine, of course, but don't feed turnips when she is milking. I have tried every way to destroy the flavor of turnips in milk, but without success. I have boiled it, put soda in it, fed the cow after milking, but it was all the same—turnip flavor unmistakable—and as we don't like our butter so flavored, I only feed turnips when the cow is dry.

The Rev. E. P. Roe in his delightful book called "Play and Profit in My Garden," says: "If a family in ordinary good circumstances, kept a separate account of the fruit and vegetables bought and used during the year, they would, doubtless, be surprised at the sum total. But if they could see the amount they could and would consume if they didn't have to buy, surprise would be a very mild way of putting it." The same rule applies to the keeping of a cow. We buy one quart a day and manage to get along with it. Our cow gives us from ten to twenty quarts a day and we make way with the greater part of it. I think with a cow and a garden one may manage to live, but life without either, according to my ways of thinking, would be shorn of many of its pleasures.

THE COW IN THE MIDDLE STATES.

BY W. L. BATTLES, GIRARD, PA.

Instead of writing on how a cow might be kept, I propose simply to tell just how we manage our cow, what we feed her, how we procure that food; in fact everything relating to her care, so that any one can go and do likewise.

"Spot," we call her, for she has a beautiful white spot in her forehead, is not a Jersey, for we can not afford to buy one at the prices at which they are held with us; nor is she a thorough-bred of any kind; yet she is a good cow, of medium size, fills a twelve-quart pail each night and morning, when her milk is in good flow, that raises a thick coat of rich cream, which, after been churned, furnishes all the butter needed for a family of six, and some to spare. Our place is small, only two acres, and a portion of this is covered by the dwelling, barn, poultry-house, etc. The fruit garden occupies about one-fourth of an acre, and from this portion nothing is grown to furnish food for "Spot." Adjoining the barn there is half an acre of the land in good grass, or mostly clover, and every spring a quart of clover seed is sown, so as fast as the old plants die out, young ones take their places. A bushel of land plaster is sown on this when the grass begins to start in the spring. This plot produces a very heavy growth of grass and clover, enabling us to cut it three times each season; about the first of June, August, and of October. A coat of fine manure is always spread over the ground immediately after each mowing. The grass is mostly cured, and makes fine hay for winter feeding. Occasionally a small portion of the crop is used green for soiling. Besides the land occupied by buildings, fruit garden, and clover plot, there remains about one acre, which we call the garden. Here are grown all the vegetables for the family's use, besides some to sell. About one-fourth of it is planted to Early Rose potatoes, and as soon as these are sufficiently ripe for use or market, they are dug, and sweet corn, in drills, for fodder, is sown upon the land. Another fourth of an acre is planted to sugar beets; the ground being very rich, the yield is always large; this last season (1879), though very dry, I harvested one hundred and seventy-eight bushels. Our cow is very fond of the beets, and I think there is nothing better to keep up a flow of milk, and they give it no bad flavor, as do turnips. An additional fourth of an acre is planted to sweet, or evergreen, corn; as fast as the corn is picked for use or market, the green stalks are cut up, run through the cutting-box, and every particle of them consumed. As soon as the corn is all harvested, the ground it occupied is thoroughly fitted and manured, and then sown to winter rye, to be used for soiling the next spring, after which the ground is again prepared for corn. The remaining fourth acre is devoted to early peas, beans, cabbages and other garden vegetables. As soon as one crop is off, the ground is prepared, and something else is almost always planted or sown; consequently, on the most of this acre, two crops are produced each season, except where sugar-beets are grown, or late cabbages, which require the whole season to mature. With the clover on the half acre, and the forage crop and roots on the acre, we have not only had sufficient food for the cow the entire season, but have also kept our family horse, with the exception of one load of oat-straw purchased for three dollars, to mix in with the fodder corn; this is hard to cure sufficiently to keep bright and sweet through the winter, but by mixing a layer of corn-fodder, and a layer of straw, it all comes out nice and bright. Besides keeping both horse and cow, we have marketed from this little farm, in berries, vegetables, butter, eggs, poultry, and one fat hog, weighing, dressed, over three hundred pounds, four hundred and sixty-eight dollars' worth of the above produce, keeping enough for our own use, and salting down one barrel of pork.

. THE BARN.

The barn is twenty-five by thirty feet, with the stable on the south side. The stall for "Spot" is five feet wide, and the floor on which she stands is five feet long, with a manger two feet wide in front, one and a half high next to the cow, and three feet next to the barn floor. She is fastened with a wide strap around her neck, attached to a chain eighteen inches long, which is fastened to a staple driven into a post at the corner of the stall adjoining the manger; this gives her room to turn her head so as to lick any portion of her body. The floor is made of two-inch plank, battened on the under side with thin boards, raised from the ground ten inches in rear and one foot in front; all the droppings and urine fall into the four-foot alley behind. This alley has a clay floor beaten perfectly solid and level. Next to the stable door is a large bin, ten by seven feet, for storing road-dust or muck; at the other end of the stable is another bin, ten by eleven feet, for storing leaves for bedding.

My great object is not only to make "Spot" comfortable, and have her stable free from all bad odors, but to save all the manure, both liquid and solid. The best absorbent is dried muck, pulverized, or road-dust from clayey roads. As it is easier to procure the latter, I generally make use of that, and always keep from two to three inches of it in the alley; this effectually absorbs all the liquid portions and all offensive odors. Twice each day this is thrown out through a window closed by a sliding shutter in the rear of the stall, under a shed, where it remains until wanted for use. In the fall I go to the woods and procure a sufficient quantity of leaves to last until spring; a liberal use of these not only makes a nice, soft, clean bed, but largely increases the quantity of manure. The stable opens into a small yard, across one corner of which runs a small brook. Each morning the cow is permitted to go out and drink; if the weather is pleasant, she is allowed to remain out an hour for exercise. She is let out the same at night, after sunset in warm weather, so that she will not be annoyed by flies. The barn is well battened, and is warm in winter; it is well ventilated by two windows, but these, in summer, are darkened by blinds, with wide slats, to keep out flies.

SYSTEM OF FEEDING.

Each morning, while "Spot" is eating her breakfast, she is well curried with a curry comb or card, and if any filth is observed on her bag or teats (which is very seldom), they are carefully washed off, if in winter, with warm water. She is never scolded nor whipped; consequently she never kicks over the pail, or holds up her milk. She is fed in winter with a peck of sugar-beets cut up, both morning, noon, and night; also a bushel of cut feed, either corn-stalks or clover hay, wet with a pailful of hot water, with two quarts of "sugar meal," or bran, thoroughly mixed together, with a little salt sprinkled over it. I generally use what is known here as "sugar meal" to mix with her feed; it is corn meal from the factory after the sugar or glucose has been extracted; it costs from ten cents to twelve and a half cents per bushel, and I prefer it to bran, and "Spot" likes it very much. We consider her a machine for converting the food we give her into milk, and the more we can get her to eat and digest, the more milk is obtained, and the greater the profit. It is a good plan to change the food occasionally, substituting carrots for beets, clover hay for corn fodder, for brutes, like mankind, are fond of a variety. There are root-cutters that can be procured for cutting up roots, but I have always used a common spade, ground sharp, and an empty flour barrel to hold the beets. It takes but a few minutes to cut up a mess of beets in that way.

MANURE.

With a bin of road-dust, and one of leaves, a winter's supply of litter is secured, and it is surprising what a pile of manure we have in the spring. Another valuable source of manure is the pigsty, with plenty of leaves for a warm bed, and sufficient road-dust to absorb all the liquids, it is astonishing how clean our pigs are, and the sty is free from all bad odors; the big potatoes and mammoth beets, show the richness of the pig-pen fertilizer. I think our fifty hens pay for all their food with the droppings the poultry-house furnishes. The roosts are over a slanting platform, which is kept covered with road-dust both summer and winter; the droppings fall on this floor, and roll down into a large box twelve feet long, three feet wide, and three feet deep. The dust the chickens work down with the droppings is sufficient to absorb all the ammonia and preserve all the fertilizing qualities of this most valuable guano. A large box of road-dust is always kept in the water-closet, a liberal use of which furnishes a quantity of most valuable fertilizer, besides freeing the closets from all noxious smells. The wash water and slops from the kitchen are utilized by being thrown on a pile of sods and other rubbish, which are forked over, and as soon as decayed, carted to the manure pile. From so many sources we are enabled to give our small farm a most liberal supply of manure each spring and fall, so that even with the double cropping most of it gets, it continues to improve, and yields more bountifully each succeeding season.

CROPS AND TILLAGE.

In the cultivation of sugar beets, the ground is first manured heavily, plowed deep, and thoroughly pulverized with the cultivator, then marked out in rows with a garden plow, two feet apart. Manure from the poultry-house is scattered in each furrow, which should be lightly covered with soil, so the seed will not come in contact with it; drop the seeds about six inches apart, covering lightly with the garden rake. When the leaves are about four inches long, thin out to one plant in a place, and fill any vacancies with the plants pulled out. Hoe them thoroughly, destroying all weeds, which can easily be done by cultivating each time before hoeing, with an arrow cultivator. Keep the ground mellow, and cultivate three or four times, after which they will take care of themselves and soon cover the ground. With ground in good condition, and a fair season, six hundred to eight hundred bushels per acre can be easily produced. Let them grow until frost comes, when they should be dug with a garden fork, the tops cut off, and stored for winter. Those to be used before the first of March, are stored in the cellar, the others are buried in a long pit, digging out a shallow place, piling up the roots about three feet high, and three feet wide, covering well with straw and sufficient soil to keep them from freezing, putting in a drain-tile about every four feet in the top of the pile, with one end to project a little through the covering, for ventilation. If the weather becomes very cold, lay a turf over the tile, and remove when pleasant. I grow carrots after the same plan, and store in like manner. I prefer beets, as they are so much larger, it is less trouble to gather and take care of them, and the crop is generally larger, still I always grow some carrots for a change. I plant sweet corn in drills, always put some fertilizer along the furrow, dropping the kernels about eight inches apart, with the rows three feet wide, I commence planting soon after May first, and continue at intervals until about July first, so I can have a fresh supply for use, and market, all the season. The sweet corn being grown on the plot sown to winter rye, for soiling, enables us to cut some portions of it twice, before the ground is needed for corn. When sowing corn for fodder, which is done as soon as we commence digging the early potatoes, I sow it in drills two feet apart, and drop the kernels about one inch apart in the drills, manure from the pigsty is first dropped in the furrow, and covered with soil at least two inches deep, or the corn will not come up. This fertilizer is so strong, if properly used it causes a most extraordinary growth of stalks. While the corn is small, cultivate it two or three times with a narrow cultivator, when it will take care of itself, and there will be a surprising growth of stalks; I have them often six feet high. Just before time for frosts, cut with a scythe, and set up in small bunches bound around the top, and leave to cure until cold weather. When it is to be put in the mow, spread alternately a layer of stalks, and a layer of straw, and it will keep bright and sweet until wanted. The rye for spring soiling is sown when the sweet corn is picked, and stalks removed, in drills about ten inches apart. Fine manure is spread on the ground after plowing, and thoroughly mixed with the surface soil; one or two hoeings being given to keep the ground mellow; to destroy any weeds that may make their appearance. By May first, the early sown rye will cover the ground with a dense growth, at least four feet high, furnishing a large quantity of most nutritious green food. On those portions of the plot where the latest corn is to be planted, two or three cuttings are made; this gives most excellent food for the cow, and the quantity grown on this fourth of an acre will surprise any one who has never tried it. There is quite a plot of early peas, and as soon as the last picking occurs, while the vines are green, they are pulled and fed to "Spot," who relishes them very much. Turnips, or corn, are at once sown on the ground where the peas were.

When our early cabbages are taken up, all the leaves, and much of the stalks, are turned into milk by taking them to the cow's manger, and the ground at once planted, or sown, to something that will make more food. The beet, carrot, and turnip tops, and late cabbage leaves, make quite a quantity of feed late in the fall, if care is taken in saving and preserving them. Possibly there may be some better forage crop than "evergreen," or sugar corn; I think another fall I will try the Minnesota Amber Sugar Cane, in a small way. I tried Pearl Millet, in one row, this season; it tillered, or spread wonderfully, but did not do so well as the corn, as the stalks were small, and the millet makes such a feeble growth, at first, it requires the whole season to produce as much fodder as I get from corn sowed the fourth of July.

CALVING.

I generally manage to have the cow come in about the first of September; by that means the six weeks time she is allowed to go dry, occurs during the warmest portion of the summer, viz., in July and August, when, with the facilities the person who keeps but one cow possesses, it is difficult to make good butter. This is also the season when butter most generally sells the lowest.

The calf is taught to drink after it is a week or ten days old, and fed on a porridge made from skim-milk and wheat middlings, or shorts; by the time it is six weeks or two months old it will be well fattened, and can be sold to the butcher for veal, at a good price, for at that season of the year veal is scarce and in demand. The cow being in full flow of milk all winter, when butter is most always high, will pay a good profit for her feed and care. A couple of weeks prior to the time the calf should be born, I make a box stall on the barn floor, and permit the cow to run loose in it until the calf is taken away to learn to drink. During this time she should have a good bed of leaves, and the stall be cleaned each night and morning. So far at such times I have experienced no difficulty, or trouble; should any occur, it is better to apply to an experienced person, than to try and "doctor" her yourself. After the calf is born, I feed the cow on warm slops a day or two, permitting the calf to suck until the swelling has gone from her bag, and it has assumed its natural condition. Then, as before stated, teach it to drink, which can easily be done by inserting the finger in its mouth, and putting its head in the dish, cautiously withdrawing the finger a few times, and in a short time you will have no difficulty, as it will help itself.

In conclusion, I can say I have tried to state just how our cow is managed and kept. I presume there can be improvements made on our system. I shall be glad to take advantage of the experience of others, at any and all times. No record is kept of the milk obtained, or of the butter made. We know we always have plenty for the family's use, and considerable to spare. Bread and milk furnish the children half their food a portion of the time. Pure milk and plenty of fresh fruits, in abundance, we consider afford one of the principal reasons why our family is so healthy, and we have so few doctor's bills to pay.

From our acre and a half, all the food has been grown for both cow and horse, except the three dollars expended for straw. The "sugar meal" given the cow has not cost five dollars during the past year. It is safe to say, that one half, and probably more, of the clover, corn fodder, green rye, etc., has been fed to the horse. Consequently the keeping of the cow can all be credited to the small area of about three-fourths of an acre of land, in addition to an outlay of not exceeding seven dollars for meal, bran, and straw. This land, about one half of it, has also produced, in addition, full crops for the use of the family, or market, while the sour milk and buttermilk have largely assisted in making six hundred pounds of pork. The calf, at less than two months of age, was sold for eight dollars, which more than paid for the extra feed bought for the cow. The family which has never kept a cow can hardly realize the satisfaction and benefits derived from such a source. Children, whose appetites are often capricious, will almost always relish a cup of cool milk. Cream, for our coffee at breakfast, is much enjoyed by all, but realized by few, and what can be more delicious than a nice dish of strawberries smothered in rich yellow cream. When we consider the small expense, the little trouble and care, contrasted with the great benefits derived, it is, so to speak, surprising that any family should rest satisfied without possessing a cow.

Fig. 2.—THE AYRSHIRE COW "OLD CREAMER."

THE COW IN THE GULF STATES.

BY GEORGE G. DUFFEE, MOBILE, ALA.

For several years I had been experimenting on a small scale in soiling cattle. My area of land, however, was exceedingly limited, being only a portion of the kitchen garden of a city residence, but my success was, even in this small way, so satisfactory, that I determined at some future day to try it on a more extensive scale. My reading and experience convinced me, that in our favored southern climate, a half acre of land, intelligently cultivated, would produce a supply of food amply sufficient to support one cow through the year, and circumstances favoring, I determined to try the experiment. In April, 1876, I became owner of a lot two hundred and fifty feet long by one hundred and twenty wide in the rear of my premises—the greater portion having been used as a grass plot for a horse. I immediately began by fencing off a portion one hundred and twenty feet by two hundred, running a wagon-way eight feet wide down the center, which, with the space occupied by the stable (say twenty by thirty feet), left nearly twenty-two thousand feet, or within a fraction of half an acre, for actual cultivation. The land was a sandy loam, covered with a thick sod of Bermuda and other grasses. Years before it had been cultivated as a market garden, but latterly given up to grass; it sloped to the south sufficiently to favor good drainage. In and around the stable was a goodly lot of manure, which, during April, was spread upon the land—some forty cart loads. On April twentieth the land was thoroughly plowed with a two-horse turning-plow, and harrowed until finely pulverized. On May first, I planted one half of the land in Southern field corn, in drills two feet apart, with the grains about one inch apart. The rows were lengthwise, to render after cultivation more convenient. On May fourth, sugar corn was put in one half of the remainder, planting at the same distance as the larger variety. May sixth, the remaining fourth was sown heavily with German or "Golden" Millet, in drills twelve inches apart. Seasonable showers, followed by warm sunny days, soon produced a vigorous and rapid growth. On May fifteenth, a Thomas' harrow was run over the first planted corn, and six days later over the second planting, and over the millet. On May thirtieth, the corn was plowed, followed by a good hoeing. A fortnight later, a second and last hoeing was given. The millet was also hoed twice, after which the growth effectually shaded the ground, and thus prevented the growth of weeds. In the meantime I had repaired the stable, and had a large door cut into the side next to the original lot, and made a stall for our pet Jersey cow. The floor was cypress, three inches thick, and sloped slightly from the manger. By actual measurement of the space occupied by the cow—giving just room for her hind feet to clear the same, a trough, eight inches deep, and fifteen wide, was made to receive the urine and droppings. The stall was four and one half feet wide, the sides coming only half the length of the cow, and just her hight. The manger extended entirely across the stall, was twelve inches wide at the bottom, and eighteen at the top, and twelve deep, the bottom being twelve inches above the floor. The fastening consisted of a five-eighths iron rod, passing from one side of the stall to the other, along the center of the manger, and one inch from it. On this rod was a ring, to which was attached a short chain that ended in a snap-catch, to attach to a ring fastened to the head-stall—the head-stall being made of good, broad leather. Usually, in turning the cow out in the morning, the head-stall was unbuckled and left in the stable; to fasten again was but a moment's work. By this arrangement the cow had full liberty to move her head, without any possibility of getting fastened by the halter. The bottom of this manger was made of slats, one half inch apart, so that no dirt could collect. For feeding wet messes, there was a box made to fit one end of the manger, which could be removed to be washed without trouble. With plenty of sawdust, costing only the hauling, perfect comfort and perfect cleanliness were matters of course.

Attached to the stable was a lot fifty by fifty feet, where, in pleasant weather, the cow was turned, but free to go in and out of her stall at pleasure. In this lot was a trough, connected with the pump, where a supply of clean and fresh water was always kept. Daily this trough was emptied and thoroughly cleaned. A cow may eat dirty feed occasionally, but see to it that the water she drinks is pure. Unless this is attended to her milk is unfit for human food.

The manure trough being supplied with sawdust, the urine, as well as the droppings, were saved and removed daily to a covered shed located in one corner of the lot, where it was kept moist, and worked over occasionally. Our Jersey was due with her second calf about June twentieth, but was still giving milk in April and May. Her feed from May first to June fifteenth, was the run of a common pasture, with a mess twice daily of wheat bran and corn meal, with hay. On June first she was dried up for a brief resting spell. June fifteenth we began cutting the sugar corn, now waist high. This was run through a cutter (making cuts three-quarters of an inch), and fed to her three times a day, first sprinkling two quarts of wheat bran over the corn, and continuing the hay feed twice a day. At the same time she was taken from the pasture, not to go on again until this experiment was finished. June twenty-second her udder was so distended, it was deemed prudent to relieve it by milking. This was done twice a day for three days. Here, at the South, there is a foolish prejudice against doing this, the belief being strong among the ignorant classes that it will cause the death of the coming calf. In some instances I have found it necessary to relieve the udder daily for a week before calving; I never knew any evil to result. At dawn June twenty-fifth there was a fine heifer calf beside her. As soon as convenient the cow was thoroughly milked, and a bucket of water, with one quart each of corn meal and wheat bran stirred in, and a pinch of salt, was given her, and nothing else except water for twenty-four hours. At evening she was again milked to the last drop, and the calf left with her during the night. Next morning a small feed of three quarts of wheat bran, and one quart of corn meal, made pretty wet, was given her, and her udder again thoroughly emptied. After milking, a small feed of hay was given, and a pail of water placed near. The calf was separated from her, but within sight. At mid-day the calf was allowed to take her fill, and afterwards the udder stripped. At evening, as the cow seemed to be free from any indications of fever, or inflamed bag, she was given a full mess of corn meal, wheat bran, cotton-seed meal, and hay. Her calf took her supper, and the udder was again stripped; that night the calf was taken from her, never to suck again, as fresh milk in a city was too valuable to feed to even a registered Jersey. Having, in years past, lost several very fine cows from over-feeding and under-milking, at calving time, I cannot urge too strongly what Col. Geo. E. Waring calls "high starvation" at this critical period in a cow's life. If a cow has been decently cared for up to the day of calving, she needs nothing but rest, quiet, and a light mash,—warm in cold weather—for twenty-four hours, and then but light feeding for two or three days. But be sure to empty her udder completely at least twice every twenty-four hours, and if the cow is a deep milker, then three times; with this treatment, the feed can be gradually increased to all that she will eat up clean.

TEACHING THE CALF TO DRINK.

It is a very easy matter to teach a calf to drink milk, when one has seen the thing done. Next morning this calf was impatient for her mess of warm milk, so, after milking her dam, I took a shallow pan, and putting two quarts of milk into it proceeded to give the first lesson in a calf's life, of doing without a mother. The process is very simple; you merely wet the first and second fingers of the left hand with milk, and place them in the calf's mouth, to give her a taste of what is in store. Repeat this a few times, then gradually draw the pan near her mouth with the right hand, using your left as above. When the calf permits your two fingers to enter her mouth, raise the pan so that your left hand will be immersed, and the calf, by suction, will draw the milk up between the fingers. At mid-day, another mess of milk, and a second lesson was given; at evening a third. Next morning the process was repeated, but in this instance she did not need the fingers to guide her to what was good for her; she readily accepted the situation, and stuck her pretty nose into the warm milk, which rapidly disappeared to where it would do the most good. But with milk worth ten cents per quart, and cream seven times as much, it did not "pay" to use six quarts daily of rich Jersey milk in this way, so, after a fortnight's supply of the raw material, the feed was gradually changed to sweet skim-milk for two weeks, and then substituting hay-tea, the milk ration was cut down to two quarts daily. Beginning with a tablespoonful of cotton-seed meal, thoroughly mixed with the feed, the quantity was increased in ten days to one pint daily. At one month old, she was gradually taught to eat bran by stirring it into her food.

The preparation of hay-tea is very simple. Nice hay is run through a cutter, and taking an ordinary two-gallon pailful, boiling water is poured upon it; it is then covered and allowed to steep for twelve hours. This makes a most excellent food, and calves thrive upon it. The most stylish and vigorous calf I ever saw, was raised upon hay-tea, with bran and cotton-seed meal as here described. I enter thus fully into the best manner of raising a calf without its mother, for the especial benefit of my southern readers, where the thriftless habit of allowing the calf to suck its dam, oftentimes until a year old, so generally prevails. In this instance the little heifer got along nicely until two months old, when an aggravated attack of scours set in, but by timely doses of laudanum in a mess of warm gruel, poured down her throat twice a day, for three days, a cure was effected. In ordinary cases of scours, a change to dry food will correct it, but it is well to watch and not to permit the disease to become seated. A few years ago, a very valuable young Jersey heifer, received from the vicinity of Philadelphia, was taken in this way, while undergoing the usual course of acclimation incident to northern cattle brought south, and the simpler treatment proving of no effect, I gave injections twice a day of rice-water and laudanum, besides drenching her with corn-gruel and laudanum. This was kept up for ten days; we carried her safely through, and her present value amply compensates for the time and trouble expended.

FOOD OF THE COW.

But let us return to the cow. On the morning of June twenty-ninth, we began giving her a fair feed of green corn, adding to it wheat bran, and cotton-seed meal. July second we fed her all the corn stalks she would eat, continuing to add bran and cotton meal, giving four quarts of the former and two of the latter; and this was her daily food, including the German Millet, treated in the same way, until September. The green food was given three times a day, but the bran and cotton meal added only morning and night. Occasionally a day's supply was cut early in the morning, and allowed to wilt before feeding, but in this, as well as in many other matters, my man-of-all-work did as circumstances permitted. His various duties about the place gave him but little time to reduce to an exact system the care and feed of a cow. She had a good stable, and plenty to eat, received daily a good brushing, and was treated kindly. Yet, she was our servant (and a most faithful one she was), and we were not her's, or slaves to any arbitrary clock-work regularity. She was fed and milked at regular intervals, but beyond this it was not always convenient to have regular hours at her stable. We did not keep her as an exhibition of a model cow in a model stable, and to exemplify a model system of care and keep. Like thousands all over the land, we kept her simply for the profit she yielded, in the way of milk and butter. It has often struck me, in reading the many suggestions and hints about how to keep a cow, to be found in some agricultural and live-stock journals, that were they all carried into practical operation, it would take the entire time of two able-bodied men to attend one animal—one to be always on hand during the day, the other to serve at night. Now common sense is a good thing, even when applied to the management of cows, and my experience convinces me that the average man wishes only to know the cheapest and easiest way to have an abundant supply of rich, wholesome, and clean milk, and with pride enough in the possession of a good cow to furnish a good shelter and comfortable quarters. Beyond these, breeders of fancy and high-priced stock may go to any extreme, and find a paying business in doing so, but the village or city owner of one or two cows, kept solely for his own use, can not afford to indulge in any of this "upper-tendom" style of cow life; it won't pay him. As a row of corn was cut and fed, the land was plowed, manured, and more corn (common field) drilled in thick, so that the ground for the whole summer presented the appearance of an experimental corn field, with corn at every stage of its growth.

This was kept up through the months of July, August, September, and October. Indeed, the half of this yield was more than sufficient for keeping the cow in superb condition, so that much the greater portion was cut in the tasselling stage and cured for winter feed. After September begins, it will not do to sow corn; the worms destroy it, but in our southern Bean, or "cow pea," we have one of the very best of soiling crops. Sown either broadcast, or in drills, it does equally well, makes a rapid growth, and affords a tempting and nutritious food for cattle. It grows until checked by frost, and I know of no plant, save Indian corn, that produces more weight to a given quantity of land. In this instance we fed it daily during October and late into November, before a frost put an end to its use in its green state. Anticipating a frost, it was cut and cured for winter feed. Properly cured, no hay equals it for cattle.

November twenty-fourth our cow went into winter quarters, and for her winter feed there were over four thousand eight hundred pounds of well cured corn-fodder, and one thousand five hundred pounds of good pea-vine hay—far more than she could consume.

Early in December, after spreading over the land all the manure on hand, it was plowed again with a two-horse turning plow, and sowed thickly to oats, harrowing them in. A seasonable rain gave them a good start, so they were well prepared for the vicisitudes of winter—a good stand and vigorous growth. The cow now received a daily ration of corn fodder and pea hay, run through the cutter, and after mixing thoroughly three quarts of wheat bran and one quart of cotton-seed meal, were wet with water (warm in cold weather). This was given her in the morning, and the same quantity at evening. The corn fodder and pea-hay for a day's feed were fifteen pounds of each, more or less. On this food she was kept through the winter, giving milk of excellent quality, and in good quantity.

In February, she was tethered every fair day in the oats, and in March, we fed her a good mess of fresh cut oats, still, however, keeping up the winter feed of corn fodder, pea-hay, wheat bran, and cotton meal. About April first, the feed of green oats was increased to all she would eat, feeding three times daily, and the excellence of this diet was shown by a marked increase in the quantity of her milk. Though due to calve again in July, she continued to supply a family of ten persons with an abundance of milk. Late in April, when the oats were in the milk state, they were cut and cured for hay, making a little over a ton of good food.

Upon summing up the result, the following dollar and cents view of the experiment of sustaining a cow on a half acre is submitted. The labor expended in cultivation is not put down as an item of expense, as the carriage horse was used in plowing, and the hired man did the rest.

Dr.
To 1,500 pounds Wheat Bran, at 90c......................$13.50
" 200 pounds Corn Meal, at 70c........................ 1.40
" 800 pounds Cotton-seed Meal, at $1................. 8.00
" 300 pounds Hay, at 75c............................. 2.25
Total...$25.15

Cr.
By sale of 2,200 pounds of Corn-fodder, at 60c....$13.20
"   "   2,100 pounds of Oats, at 75c............ 15.75
$28.95
Profit..$ 3.80

But the profit above shown does not express the real profit. A year's continuous supply of rich milk in abundance, for a large household, cream for special occasions, and that best of luxuries, delicious home-made butter, and one hundred dollars for the little heifer when six months old, aggregate the chief results of the experiment.

For the best results in soiling, no crop compares, as far as my experience goes, with our Southern variety of Indian corn; on rich land it produces marvellously. I have raised it at the rate of one hundred thousand pounds (or fifty tons) per acre. There is no difficulty in producing three crops in one season on the same land. But cattle need a variety of food in soiling, as in other forms of feeding. Oats are excellent, and come in early. Cat-tail Millet ("Pearl Millet") is a rapid grower, but cattle are not specially fond of it; they like German Millet better. Garden (or

English) Peas make an excellent food, coming into use in March, and lasting to June. I remember one year I produced five crops for soiling, on the same land, in one year, namely: oats, three of corn, and one of cow-peas. The last named is a superb food late in the year, after corn has gone. I have never experimented with roots, nor am I aware of any being cultivated in the South as a soiling crop. Cabbages set out in September and October will be ready for feeding in December, and will, next to corn, produce the largest weight of green food. One year I fed them to a considerable extent, and found my cows were very partial to them. By beginning with cabbages in December, to be succeeded by oats in March, then peas, corn, and millet, to wind up in November with cow-pea, a cow in our climate can be soiled every day in the year.

Fig. 3.—THE JERSEY COW "ROSALEE."

THE VILLAGE COW IN NEW ENGLAND.
BEING THE JOURNAL OF THE KEEPER.
BY HENRY E. ALVORD, EASTHAMPTON, MASS.

In writing upon this subject the narrative form is convenient, and while it cannot be claimed that this is entirely a " true story," it may be said to be founded on fact. Personal experience is my basis, and whatever of fancy may be interwoven with the facts would have been quite practicable, and all ought to have occurred as narrated, if all did not.

Let me premise by saying that I own a comfortable little home in a village of a few thousand inhabitants, not a thousand miles from New York, supporting my family by a moderate income earned from day to day, and my occupation is such as to enable me to spend an average of three hours of daylight on my place, from the middle of March to the middle of October, and occasionally a whole day besides. Thus I can make and care for my garden, which for some years has uniformly been an excellent one, quite a model, though I say it. Of this sort of work I have always been very fond, as well as of domestic animals, all kinds of which were familiar to me when a boy.

MAY 1ST, 1875.—For several years I have kept more or less poultry, and sometimes a pig; there is so much from a good garden that is otherwise wasted. The ambition of the family is to own a horse and a cow. It has been talked about a good deal, but we are agreed that the horse would be a pure luxury, in our circumstances, and must wait. The cow I have felt would be a luxury too, that is, cost more than it would produce, but on this point the good wife has differed with me, claiming that it would be a real economy. It has been a part of our domestic policy to use milk and butter liberally, thereby keeping down the butcher's bill and buying very little lard. Of the value of milk as an article of food, in its natural state, and in the many ways which it can be used in cooking, there can be no doubt, especially where there are young and growing members of the family. Still, I have been skeptical on the economy of keeping a cow, and to convince me, the help-meet recently proved, from well kept accounts, that during the last two years there have been consumed by our family of five persons, one thousand five hundred and forty-five quarts of milk, averaging seven cents a quart, and three hundred and sixty-one pounds of butter, average price thirty-three cents a pound,

These have amounted to a cash expenditure of one hundred and thirteen dollars and sixty-four cents a year, which was a decided surprise to me, and feeling pretty sure the expense need not exceed two dollars a week, I yielded to the argument; am the owner of a cow, and here record the result of my experiment. One of the pleasant spring days of last week, we took a drive among the farms of the vicinity, and selected a good looking cow which had just dropped her second calf. The price paid was sixty-five dollars, to be delivered to me to-day, without the calf. The man I bought of called her "pure Alderney," but she looks large of her age for that race, weighing somewhat over seven hundred pounds, and if, two or three generations back there was a cross of Ayrshire, or of Guernsey, it is all the better. My belief is that she has a streak of Ayrshire blood, and that she will make a fine cow. Being three years old next month (exact date unknown), it has been decided that our cow is to be known as "June."

MAY 1ST, 1876.—When "June" was bought, it was in the full expectation that pasturage could be hired in a small lot adjoining the rear of mine. I supposed it was fixed, but the spring had been favorable, the grass on the meadow promised well, and the owner concluded he would mow it, so that arrangement fell through. By that time I was too late to secure room in the only pasture convenient to the village, and I have been forced to keep her in the stable and a small stable yard, the whole year. The result is more than satisfactory, considering the disadvantageous circumstances.

A year ago to-day "June" arrived, in fair condition, save that her coat looked a little rough, and with a good bag of milk; her daily yield that month was about twelve quarts. In a day or two I noticed that when in the yard, she rubbed her neck vigorously against the corner of the stable and sometimes backed up to a building or fence for the purpose. An examination proved that she had vermin upon her; so I made a pail full of strong suds, with soft soap, and put into it an ounce of sulphuric acid, and with this I sponged the parts infested, twice daily, for a few days. This seemed efficient and there has been no such trouble since.

For long forage "June" had only dry food, good fine hay, until late in May, and then I began to give her a green bite whenever I could, clippings from the yard, trimmings of early vegetables and whatever there was to spare from the garden. Besides this, everything she ate had to be bought, except a few roots used since February. A little bran was fed for the first few days, and gradually increased, so that during the summer she received four pounds daily, fed in two parts, morning and night. Later in the season corn-meal was added to the ration, and at times oats were substituted for the bran. In the winter, eight pounds of meal and bran, half and half, mixed, was the daily allowance. Buying hay in small quantities I managed to keep both rowen and clover hay on hand, some of it very fresh, and could thus vary the dry food. Also, for variety, I frequently gave one cut feed a day, moistened. Besides this, I obtained and worked in, during the summer, a lot of half-ripe oats, in the straw, which had lodged and were cured like hay. The food, although thus often changed, was changed carefully.

In my garden I made a large parsnip bed, and followed my earliest peas with carrots, so that in the fall there were several bushels of these roots. The carrots were buried in the garden, a mellow loam, and the parsnips left in the ground. The former were opened during a thaw in February, and a few fed to "June" each day, lasting until the end of March; by that time I could get the parsnips and they have just given out. When I began the roots the grain was gradually withheld and she has had none since February. These roots have had a most apparent effect, giving her coat a bright, thrifty look, and she is in fine condition for calving, which is expected in ten days. But the roots made it hard to dry off the cow. She was shrinking in milk fast when we began on the carrots, then started up again and was giving about three quarts a day in March, when the milk (and especially the cream) began to have a sharp, unpleasant, bitter taste, and we soon had to give up using it. It then took a fortnight to dry her off, which was done by lessening the roots, milking not quite dry, then only once a day, and once in two days. Water has been offered three times a day, through the year, all she would drink, salt has always been within her reach. All summer, and every mild, dry day in winter, "June" has passed some hours in the stable yard. A large amount of bedding has been necessary, and for this I have used the waste hay, the rakings of the yard last autumn, the scrapings of the garden walks, garden litter, and the leaves from a row of maple trees in front of the house, carefully saved for the purpose. So much in the stall, "June" has required more personal care, and it has been made a rule to rub and brush her body enough to keep it clean and free from dead skin. But I never use a harsh card; nothing is better for rubbing than a piece of old seine or very coarse bagging. Everything about the cow, too, is kept clean and sweet.

The result of this continuous stabling has been a rapid accumulation of manure, and this having been mixed with all the suitable refuse of the place, and forked over several times, I this spring have on hand a huge pile of rich compost. It is more than can be used on the garden, and the newer part has been corded up under a temporary shed for sale or future use. This alone well pays for all my extra work in keeping the cow, as I have yearly been obliged to buy for the garden.

Our plan during the year has been to sell a little milk to neighbors, set aside two quarts daily for family use, cream and all. The cream from the remainder has been made into butter, and an accurate account kept of the butter produced.

The following is the result of this first year keeping one cow:

EXPENSES:		RETURNS:	
Interest 7 per cent on cost of cow.	$ 4.53	155 qts. Milk sold @ 7c	$ 10.85
4 tons of Hay, av. $20	80.00	311 qts. Skim-milk, @ 3c	9 33
500 lbs Oats in straw	4.25	Sales	$ 20.18
960 lbs. Wheat Bran, @ $1.20	11.52	620 qts. Milk for family, @ 7c	43.40
350 lbs. Corn-Meal @ $1.10	3.85	123 lbs. Butter made, @ 35c	43.05
4 bus. Oats @ 55c	2.20	Year's return	$106.63
Expended	$106.37		
Less 400 lbs. Hay on hand	3.00	Memorandum—Cost	$103.37
Year's expense	103.37	Less sales	20.18
			83.19
		Plus purchases—	
		88 qts. Milk	6.16
		52 lbs. Butter	16.64
		Cow products cost family	$105.99

Here is a net balance of three dollars and twenty-six cents in favor of the cow, without allowing anything for the abundant supply of skim-milk and butter-milk which has been profitably used in the poultry yard as well as at the house—or for the big compost heap, which could readily be sold.

The figures also show that the family has had a better supply of cow products than last year, at seven dollars and sixty-five cents less expense. No labor is charged, for I am not so much keeping an exact account of the maintenance of the cow, as of the profit of my keeping one, taking care of her myself. And no credit is given for manure, as I mean to apply that to reducing the cost of keeping in the future. The cow might have been fed at less cost, but I intended to have her improve on my hands, and she has done so. "June" now weighs seven hundred and sixty-two pounds, is about to have her third calf, and is certainly worth more than was paid for her.

Altogether, in spite of unfavorable conditions there is no occasion to complain of the result of the year.

KEEPING ONE COW.   39

MAY 1ST, 1877.—Last spring, my neighbor, north, was willing to let me have his acre and a half of meadow for pasturage, but wanted thirty-five dollars for the season. I would not pay that, and, instead, hired a place for "June" in a large pasture half a mile or more distant, paying twenty dollars for the season, May fifteenth, to October fifteenth, and four dollars to a boy for driving. On the ninth of May, the cow dropped a bull calf without difficulty, and I gave it away the next day. No special care was needed or given, except a little caution as to feeding, and on the fifteenth the cow went to pasture. She did remarkably well until early in July, being in pasture during the day, and at the stable at night. Then the weather grew very hot, the pasture dry, and "June" began to fail rapidly in her milk; so I commenced feeding a little bran, and offered hay when she came up at night. Later, a friend recommended cotton-seed meal, and a hundred weight of that was obtained and fed with good results, two or three pounds a day. August was a month of intense dry heat, and the pasture became of little use except for the exercise, shade, and water. In spite of meal and hay fed at night, "June's" yield of milk shrank to three quarts a day, and we feared she would go dry. August fifth, I made the change of sending her to pasture just before six o'clock in the evening, as the boy went after the other cows, and bringing her up to the stable in the morning, where I kept her during the day. This was an improvement, and also gave better opportunity of feeding sweet corn-stalks, vegetable trimmings and the like, fresh from the garden. The grain was continued through August, and she ate more or less hay. At the end of the month she was giving over a gallon of milk a day. Rains came early in September, the pasturage soon became good again, and the daily mess of milk steadily increased until November. By that time she was in the stable for the winter, and the treatment since has been practically a repetition of last year. My root patch in the garden was enlarged, as the result of last year's experience, and accordingly I put eight or ten bushels of carrots into my cellar in October, covering them with sand, and left a fine lot of parsnips in the ground. I began feeding the carrots in January, two or three a day, just for a relish; gradually increased them, until in February the cow received half a peck or more, and thus they lasted into March. Then I dried her off, getting the last milk to use March twenty-eighth. Grain feeding was stopped the first of March, and she has had none since. After the cow was fully dry, I began on the parsnips, and she is now getting half a peck daily, with all the hay she will eat. "June" will be fresh again on the twentieth of this month.

The season has not satisfied me. Not only has the weather been unfavorable, (we must expect severe summers occasionally,) but I don't like sending the cow to a distant pasture which I can know very little about, and where nobody knows how the other animals treat her. I shall never do this again if any other arrangement can be made.

The account for the year is as follows:

EXPENSES.		RETURNS.	
Interest at 7 per cent. on cost of cow	$4.55	42 qts Milk sold at 6½c	$2 73
Hay from last year	3.00	286 qts. Skim-milk sold at 3c	8.58
2½ tons Timothy Hay @ $18	45.00	Sales	$11.31
Pasturage and driving	24.00	640 qts. Milk for family, at 6½c	41.60
750 lbs. Wheat Bran @ $1.10	8.25	109 lbs. Butter made @ 32c	34.88
430 lbs. Corn-Meal @ $1	4.50	Year's returns	$87.79
100 lbs. Cotton-seed Meal	2.00	Memorandum—Cost	$89.30
Expended	$91.30	Less sales 11.31	77.99
Less hay on hand	2.00	Plus purchases—	
Year's expense	$89.30	86 qts. Milk @ 6½c	$ 5.59
		70 lbs. Butter @ 30c	21.00
		Cow products cost family	$104.58

Comparing this with last year's statement, it will be seen that although there is a small balance against the cow, she is still, all things considered, a profitable part of the domestic establishment.

MAY 1ST, 1878.—Dissatisfied with the last year's management, and seeing that there would last spring be a large surplus of fine compost on hand, more profitable to use than to sell, I planned a new arrangement in the autumn of 1876 for keeping my one cow. First, I secured the meadow west of my lot, renting it from the owner from October first, 1876, until April first, this year, for thirty dollars. The acre and a half yielded about two tons of hay in 1876, but no rowen; the aftermath was good, however, when I came in possession. The south end of it, although in good heart, was weedy and uneven. I drove some strong stakes, and ran a wire fence across, in continuation of my southern boundary, thus cutting off just about a quarter of an acre in rear of my neighbor, south. This piece I dressed with compost made the summer just preceding, and had it plowed and cross-plowed before the ground froze, in preparation for a root crop. The soil is a deep, mellow, sandy loam, but rich. Last spring the new root patch was plowed once, well dressed from the compost pile of 1875-6, and that harrowed in. (There was enough of the same compost for my garden, and to spare, so last June there was still on hand the manure of about a year's collection put up in good shape.) The rest of the work I was able to do myself. My root-garden, laid out in rows running north and south, was divided as follows: eight square rods of parsnips next to neighbor, south, on the slope, where they caught the wash from his garden; twelve square rods of carrots and ten rods of mangolds; in the point west to the stream I put sweet corn at first, and followed it with strap-leafed turnips, ten square rods. Without going into the details of root-culture, which any one who has made a good garden knows all about, I put into my house cellar last fall fifty-two bushels of Long Orange Carrots, and over forty bushels of Long Yellow Mangel Wurzels (these monstrous, twisted, forked roots are awkward things to measure, but there must have been a ton or more in weight), left in the ground from twenty to twenty-five bushels of Hollow-crowned Parsnips, and harvested thirty-six bushels of English Turnips. This was more than I had bargained for. I see now that roots enough might have been raised in my old garden, and the parsnips would have done much better there, but I sold twenty bushels each of carrots and turnips for more than enough to cover all expenditures for seed and hired labor.

A year ago to-day, I turned "June" into her new pasture of an acre and a quarter; the grass was then starting well, and I preferred to have the change gradual. She ate more or less hay until the end of the month. Doors and gates were so fixed that she could be in stall, yard, or pasture at pleasure, and could drink at the stream bordering the meadow.

CALVING AND AFTER-TREATMENT.

On the eighteenth of May, her bag began to swell, and became feverish. A quart or two of watery milk was drawn at intervals of eight hours for the next three days, and the udder was bathed as often in tepid water, and gently but thoroughly rubbed with goose oil, in which camphor-gum had been dissolved. Each day, also, she was given a quarter of a pound of Epsom Salts, dissolved in a quart of "tea" made from poke-weed root (*Phytolacca decandra*), which all druggists now keep in store; this was administered as a "drench," from a bottle, her head being held up while she swallowed it. On the morning of the twenty-second, being two days overdue, she calved, having a hard time, but producing without help a fine large heifer. Very soon after, I gave her a bucket of cool (not cold) water, in which was stirred a quart of wheat bran, a half pound of linseed-meal, previously scalded, and a handful of pulverized poke or garget root. This mess was repeated at noon, and the bag milked dry. A little later, the after-birth naturally passed off and was removed. The udder remained hot, knotty, and so tender that when the calf sucked I had to protect it from the mother's kicks, and also to prevent it from taking one teat which was extremely sore. From this quarter I carefully drew the milk with one of a set of four "milking-tubes," which I bought two years ago to do my milking, but soon discarded; here they came in use, just the thing wanted, but one as good as four. At night I milked dry, gave a dose of half a pound of Salts, with one ounce of Nitre, and a warm Bran-mash. The bag was well rubbed as before. The cow ate some hay during the night, and a few cabbage sprouts in the morning. That day (twenty-third), she was on the pasture a little while, and had a full bag of milk, but still hot and tender. The calf was separated from the cow at daylight, and allowed to suck four times during the day, the bag being milked dry, and then oiled and well rubbed every time. The bowels appearing to be in a sufficiently active state, appetite improving, and her eyes natural, the physic was discontinued, the cow allowed to eat grass and hay at will, and for several days the calf sucked at daylight, noon, and dark, the milk left by it being all drawn. The bag was rubbed and anointed two or three times a day, and a little extract of Belladonna added to the oil used. Under this treatment the inflammation gradually subsided. As soon as the cow would allow her calf to take the tenderest teat, I kept it on that side as much as possible while sucking. At the end of a week after calving, the udder was again in sound condition. The calf was kept until the first of June, and then the owner of its sire took it in full for service of bull three seasons. We then began to get the full flow of milk, and the pasture being good, it was a fine mess daily. At that time, I began to measure the milk, and have done so ever since. "June" gave four hundred and eighty-two quarts the month she was five years old, an average of sixteen quarts a day.

Until the last of July, the cow got all her food from the pasture, and one acre would have done as well as one and a quarter. For the next five or six weeks, the grass was hardly sufficient; it was, for this period, based upon the experience of August, 1876, that the corn had been provided. The ten rods of Mammoth Sweet, three hundred and fifty to four hundred hills, had been put in at five different plantings, a week apart, and the earliest was just forming ears the last of July when I began using it, at first once a day, then twice. For each feed, the whole plants of three or four hills were taken, and chopped in a straw-cutter, ears and all, into two-inch lengths. This was eaten with great relish, and during August the cow spent most of the daytime standing in the stream where shaded by trees and grazed at night. The pasturage improved again before the corn gave out, so quite a nice piece of winter fodder was saved from the piece. Then all through September there was every day more or less of green-corn husks, carrot and beet tops, other vegetable and fruit trimmings, clean refuse from house and garden, good food for the cow, so that again one acre of pasture would have sufficed. During October, the carrots and mangolds were harvested, and their tops gave the cow more than she could manage. I also began feeding turnips the last of October, a few with mangel tops at first, increasing until she ate more than half a bushel a day, tops and all. Before the ground froze, the turnips were piled in the barn, without trimming, and covered with hay; were kept safely until the last were fed, November twenty-eighth. The problem of winter feeding really came up the first of November. I had a large supply of roots on hand of my own raising, and the hay and grain to buy. So I went to the books, and after studying both practice and science, decided upon the following daily rations for the next six months: November first to May first, fifteen pounds of meadow rowen and clover hay, in about equal parts; one pound each of coarse wheat bran and corn-meal, mixed. During November, one-half bushel turnips and two pounds cotton-seed meal; December and January, one-half bushel carrots and one and one-half pound cotton-seed meal; February and March, one-half bushel (or more) of mangels and one pound cotton-seed meal; April, one-half bushel parsnips and one and one-half pounds cotton-seed meal; also, one hundred pounds additional hay, and my corn-stalks, for February and March.

This plan has been carried out with little variation. Of course the food has not been accurately weighed daily. The grain portions, kept in barrels, have been dipped out with tin cups, but have held out just about as expected; the quantity of hay and roots has been guessed at.

THE METHOD OF FEEDING

and other work at the stable during the winter has been this: Between six and seven o'clock A. M. stall cleaned, cow brushed off, bedding and absorbents fixed, the milking done, and then a feed of six or seven pounds of chaffed hay, slightly moistened, and the bran and meal mixed with it. After this, a bucket of water left in the stall, except in the coldest weather. The bucket is fixed near the feed-box, so it can not be tipped over, and it has generally been found empty at noon. At that hour, the regular watering, two or three pailfuls, and then a small bunch of hay thrown in the box; the stall cleaned also. Between six and seven at night, the milking done and bedding fixed, the roots fed, chopped up pretty fine with a spade, and the cotton-seed meal sprinkled over them. Hay then given, and the cow left for the night.

It was my intention to feed the roots in two parts, morning and night, and I should have preferred this, but my time in the morning was limited. Preparing the roots over night, they sometimes froze, but I could cut the hay at evening, ready for the morning chop-feed. As one kind of root was about to give out, some of the next to be fed were mixed in, and thus sudden changes avoided. The extra hay and stalks calculated for February and March were not used exactly in those months, but consumed during severely cold and windy spells, being added to the usual noon and night portions. At all times, the cow had, under this plan, full as much as she was ready to eat up clean. The hay left on hand a year ago was all used last summer, and before November a full load each of the best rowen and clover hay were put into the barn, one thousand six hundred and one thousand four hundred pounds respectively, and there is a little left.

It ought also to be mentioned that while the cow was mainly fed on sweet corn, last July and August, I was obliged to add about two pounds of cotton-seed meal a day, to give quality to the milk; it was fed dry, at noon. As soon as the feeding of carrot tops began, this meal was omitted, but it was again needed when turnips were substituted for carrot and beet tops. The ration of mangolds was increased to about two bushels in three days, because there were plenty of them, and my house cellar being rather warm, they commenced to rot. I was very careful to give the cow only sound roots. This extra food in February and March resulted in a better milk record by "June" than in the two months next preceding. I shall feed more roots the coming year. There were more parsnips than could be well used; they were not needed until April, and I sold five dollars' worth, as an offset to what the cow got from last year's kitchen garden. The cow goes on to pasture to-day.

Therefore, in review, the cow has been carried through the year with the one and one-half acres rented for thirty dollars, and forty-five dollars expended for hay and grain. Against the manure taken for my garden may be placed the cleanings of the poultry house, the contents of the earth-closet, and the garden refuse and bedding, all of which go into the compost heap. The item of labor alone remains, and as all that has been hired (including the plowing of the garden) was paid from sales of surplus roots, no further account is taken of that; my own time was well spent, as the balance sheet shows. Last August, we fully determined that it would be better for the family cow to be fresh in September than in the spring. The heat of summer is the time when it is most difficult to keep a cow properly fed for a good flow of rich milk on a little place like this. It is the time when milk is plenty and cheap, if one wants to buy, and most difficult to manage or dispose of if one has much on hand. It is almost impossible to make good butter in dog-days, living as we do, with no special appliances, and it is not worth while for us to get a patent creamer and a supply of ice. In the spring, we don't want a dry cow, but are willing to have one in August. July, with its increasing heat and decreasing pasturage, is a favorable time to dry off a cow. The keeper of one cow can not afford to have her dry more than six weeks in the year, and may manage to have this period four weeks, or even less. Accordingly, I have arranged for "June" to come in next September, and shall in future practice "winter-dairying." Indeed, we have done so the past season, for with liberal feeding of a succulent character, the cow has held out well in her milk. She is now giving between five and six quarts a day, while not yet on grass, and her total yield for eleven months, since June first (or rather for the year), is found to be two thousand seven hundred and forty-six quarts. Here is my third year's annual account with "June:"

EXPENSES.		RETURNS.	
Interest at 7 per cent. on cost of cow	$ 4.55	685 qts. Milk sold at 6c	$41.10
Rent of 1¼ acres of land	30.00	464 qts. Skim-milk sold at 2¼c	11.60
Hay left from last year	2 00	Sales	$52.70
1¼ tons of Hay bought	28.50	670 qts. Milk used @ 6c	40.20
350 lbs. of Cotton-seed Meal and freight	6.80	127 lbs. Butter made @ 30c	38.10
159 lbs. Corn-Meal	1.50	Year's return	$131.00
200 lbs. Bran @ $1.15 per cwt	2.30	Memorandum—	
Year's expense	$75 65	Cost keeping $75.65	
		Less sales 52.70	$22.95
		Plus purchases—	
		55 qts. Milk @ 6c	3.30
		53 lbs. Butter @ 30c	15.90
		Cow products cost family	$42.15

An absolute profit of fifty-five dollars from the cow is shown, and a still larger saving in family expenses, besides nine hundred quarts of skim-milk and butter-milk used in the house and poultry-yard and given away. The yield of the cow shows "June" to be a superior animal, and that is what the keeper of one cow should have, for it costs little more in food and care than an ordinary one. But if the cow had been only of medium quality and no new

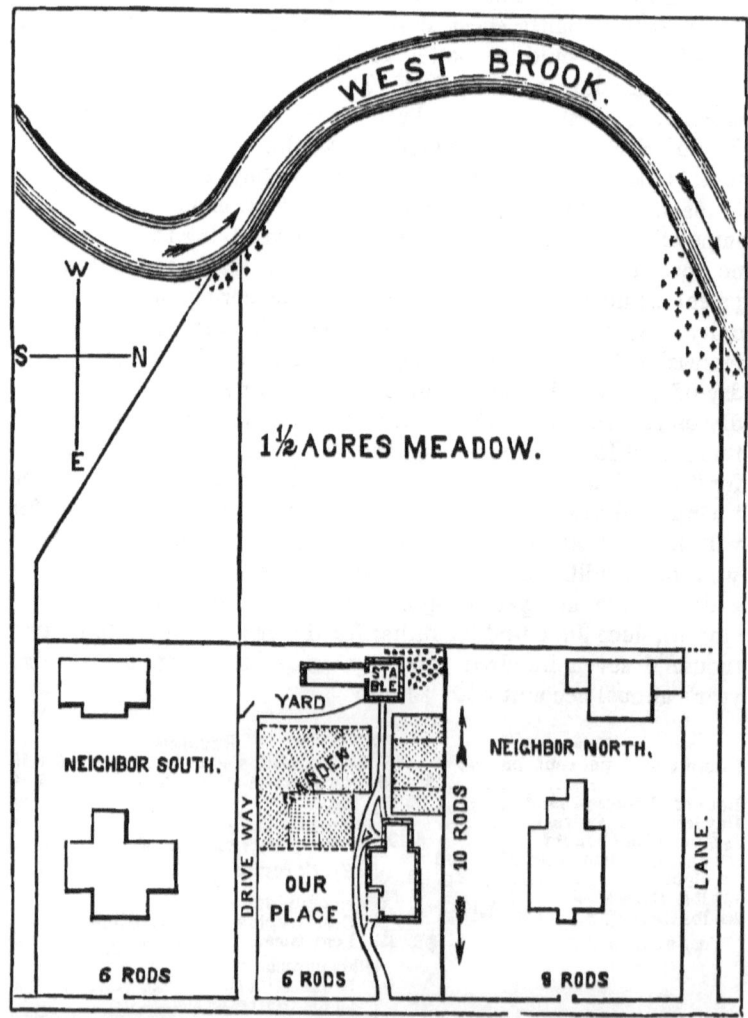

Fig. 4.—PLAN OF VILLAGE LOT AND SURROUNDINGS.

milk could be sold, it would have been a profitable operation. And if, instead of selling new milk, as much butter had been made as possible, there would still have resulted a balance of over twenty dollars in favor of the cow.

KEEPING ONE COW.   47

May 1st, 1880.—(To come within the required limits of this paper the journal of the last two years must be condensed. Therefore, omitting detailed descriptions, the general facts are given, and some opinions derived from the five years recorded.) For the year ending May, 1879, the method of keeping "June" was much the same as in that last described, but more roots were raised and fed; some hay was made, and only straw and grain food purchased. The result was even better than that shown by the last account. During the year just ended, the fifth since "June" was bought, I tried soiling, keeping the cow in stall and yard almost all the time, and have actually got through without buying hay or straw, using only one acre and a quarter to produce all the long forage needed. There is so much left over that I am satisfied one acre well managed, the preparation beginning the previous fall, can be made to support my cow, with the exception of the grain food and part of the roots. But this requires more time for labor than I can give, and more manure than one cow makes. I have had to buy fertilizers during the last two years, and although they were good, I prefer hereafter to buy food and make manure, rather than buy manures to make food. For one situated as I am, a semi-soiling system, or limited pasturage helped out with other food, is better, even if more food is bought. I can be surer of what I purchase, and thus use the one cow to better advantage.

Fig. 5.—East end of stable in 1870.

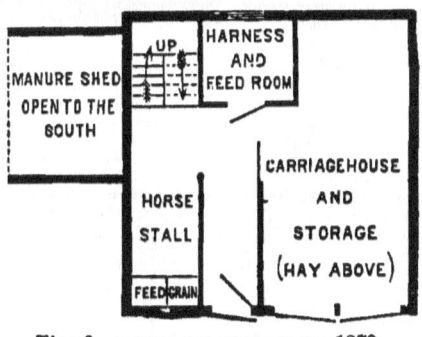

Fig. 6.—Plan of stable in 1870.

The only secret of home-made manure is to save everything, especially all liquids, mix everything as already explained, fork over

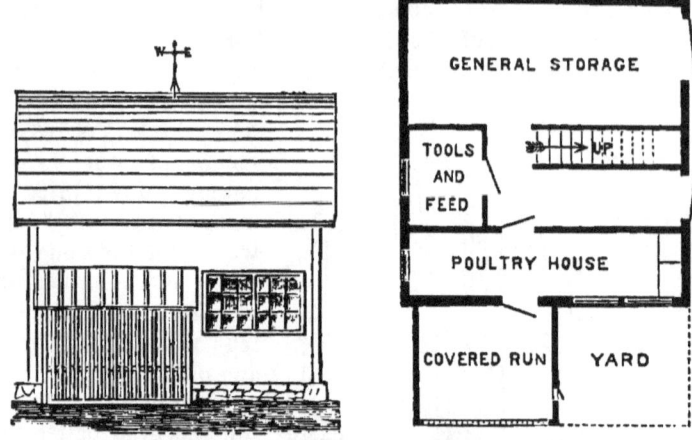

Fig. 7.—SOUTH SIDE OF STABLE AS ADAPTED FOR POULTRY IN 1871-5.

Fig. 8.—PLAN OF STABLE, 1871-5.

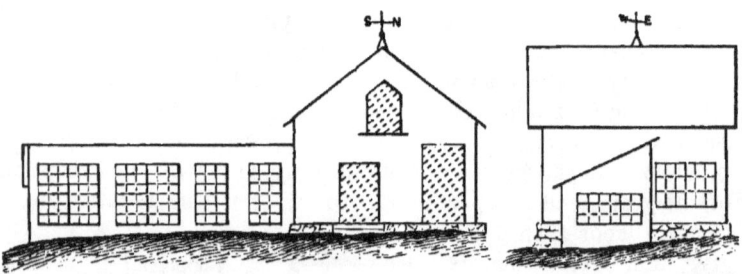

Figs. 9 and 10.—EAST AND SOUTH ELEVATIONS OF STABLE, AS CHANGED FOR POULTRY AND COW IN 1875.

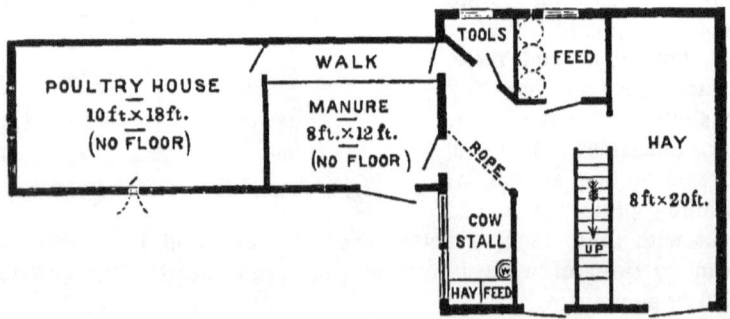

Fig. 11.—MAIN FLOOR PLAN AS CHANGED FOR COW IN 1875.

and keep compact, to make a homogenous compost, and keep all under cover until used. A very slight and cheap protecting shed will suffice.

As to housing, I began with a plain frame stable found upon

Fig. 12.—FRONT ELEVATION AS CHANGED IN 1878.

the place, made originally for one horse and a buggy, and have gradually changed and added to it, doing most of the work myself, until a very satisfactory building has resulted. It contains room

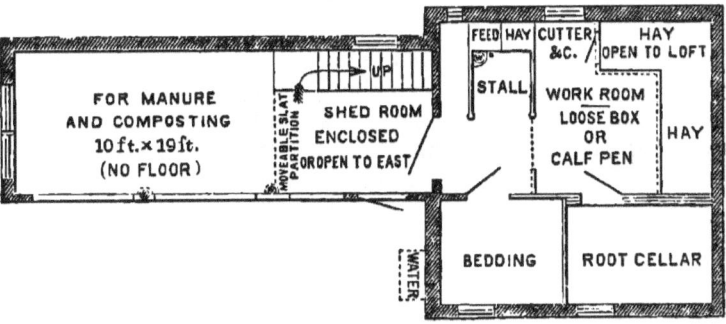

Fig. 13.—PLAN OF BARN BASEMENT WITH NEW STONE FOUNDATIONS, 1878.

enough for a year's forage, including root-cellar, a warm, dry stall, conveniently arranged for saving labor, ample shed-room for compost, and a sheltered yard containing five or six square rods, which is as good as more. There is running water in the yard. The plans accompanying this article, figs. 5 to 13 inclusive, show these arrangements better than any description in writing.

"June" had her fifth calf September sixth, 1878, and her sixth exactly a year later. At the fifth calving there was a "false presentation," and a very serious time. No competent veterinarian was within reach, or else one would have been called. As it was, I looked up the subject in back volumes of agricultural papers and other publications, went to work myself, and getting the calf into proper position, succeeded in effecting a delivery without serious consequences. Last September's calf was a heifer, and by a fine sire, so, as "June" has reached her prime, if not passed it, I am raising this calf to make a new cow to succeed the worthy dam. Most keepers of one cow, however, are so situated that they had better dispose of calves at once. Making veal is not as profitable as making butter, and feeding skim-milk to children and chickens.

In order to have the products of the cow perfectly satisfactory, I lay great stress upon the utmost care and cleanliness in milking. First, see that the stall and all about it is in order, pure air, and no dust flying, and the udder and flank of the cow quite clean. Except in the coldest weather, the udder is sponged off with tepid water, and wiped dry, just before milking. Then I trust no one to milk for me, but do it myself, quietly, quickly, and completely, milking into a funnel, which carries the fluid to a covered pail, which serves also a seat. This new and truly "Perfect" milking-pail, which I first saw described in the AMERICAN AGRICULTURIST, is a great improvement on all open vessels. I prefer not to have the cow eating while I milk; she should give her whole attention to the operation, as well as the milker. This certainty that my milk reaches the house absolutely pure, not only satisfies us as to our own cream and butter, but makes "June's" milk in great demand in the neighborhood. Our neighbors so much prefer it to milkmen's milk that they are willing to send to the house for it, and pay more than the usual village price. This adds materially to the profit of keeping one cow.

Fig. 14.—THE GUERNSEY COW "LADY JANE" AND HEIFER.

JOSEPH EARNEST AND HIS COW "COMFORT."

A STORY OF THE WESTERN RESERVE.

BY S. D. MORRIS, CHARLESTOWN, PORTAGE CO., O.

The luxury of having fresh milk, cream, and butter, may be enjoyed by every family in city, town, or hamlet, that can provide a cow with the necessaries expressed in one word—comfort. To show what may be done in this respect, allow me to give somewhat of the history of Joseph Earnest. Joseph's father was a carpenter, and never kept a horse or cow. After giving his son the best education he could receive at the common school, he kept him at work with himself until Joseph also became a master carpenter. At the time our story commences, he is married and has a family of three children, a girl of eight, a boy of six years, and a baby. By industry, economy, and good habits, he had accumulated sufficient means to purchase a half-acre lot in the outskirts of a flourishing manufacturing town. Upon this lot he had built a small but comfortable house. His wife, the daughter of a well-to-do farmer, having a little property of her own, invested it in the vacant lot adjoining them. The winter previous Joseph had put up a building which was to serve the double purpose of barn and workshop. The barn for his visiting friends, the workshop for himself. Back of this building, and adjacent to it, was a small hennery in which were kept a few fowls; at one side was a shed for his gardening implements. Everything about the premises showed the owner was neat and orderly, as well as thrifty, while within the snug cottage the same virtues reigned supreme. Many a time did Mary look back to the old home-life on the farm, and think of the plentiful products of the dairy. Then she would say to Joseph, "How I wish we could keep a cow. It seems as though I cannot half cook with only one quart of milk a day, and the children would be so much healthier if they could have what milk they want." Joseph agreed with her, and would add, "But you know Mary we cannot raise our own vegetables and fruit, and keep a cow, with only one acre of land." Imagine her surprise, when, after a short absence one morning, Joseph returned leading a cow. He was soon surrounded by his family and plied with questions, such as: Whose is she? Where did you get her? What will you do with her? In answer to these questions Joseph replied, "I went over to Mr. Durham's this morning, to see if he could pay me what was back on the work I did for him last fall. I found him feeding his cattle and made known my errand. He said he had no money at present, but was wanting to sell a cow, and as soon as he could would pay me. I asked him which cow he wanted to sell; he pointed out this one, which was smaller than the others and seemed driven by them. Not a very large cow, he said, but young, with some Jersey blood in her—better for a family cow than for a factory cow. I say Earnest, she is just what you need, with your family. But I've no place to put her, said I, and I don't know how to take care of a cow. Nonsense, said he, put her in your stable for the present, and you'll learn how to take care of her fast enough. But what shall I feed her? Why the money you pay Churchill for milk, with what you can raise on your lot, will keep your cow right along, and instead of one quart a day, you'll have all the milk and cream and butter you want to use, and some to spare, and, Mary, I thought it would'nt break us up if it didn't prove a success, so I took the cow on what he was owing me—twenty-five dollars—and here she is."

"Oh, Joseph, I am so glad you bought her, I do believe we can keep her," said Mary, "how gentle she seems,"—for during the talk the children had been petting the cow, who appeared well pleased with her new acquaintances. The baby partaking of the general animation, crowed with delight, as though already anticipating the good time coming.

"She has behaved like a baby coming over here," said Joseph, "and I declare I begin to love her already. I have always wished we could live where we could have animals around us, and perhaps we will some day." Mary said she hoped they could, for she felt lonesome for them. "But what shall we name our cow? For my part I would like to call her 'Comfort,' and while she contributes to our comfort we will endeavor to do the same for her." Joseph agreed to the name, saying he needed plenty to eat and drink, a good bed and pleasant home, and he believed that animals did too, so he would give her one of his nice roomy stalls in his barn, make her a bed of shavings from the shop until he could do better. "We have pure water for her to drink, with hay and vegetables to eat, and that will keep her alive until we learn what she will thrive on best." As this was a "broken" day, he thought they had better get neighbor Manning's horse and carry-all, and drive out to father Granger's. He had always been a good farmer and could tell him just how to care for the cow. All were delighted with this plan and were soon enjoying a six-mile drive into the country.

KEEPING ONE COW.

He learned that a cow would eat almost anything that grows, but that judgment and experience was needed in feeding to produce the best results. Father Granger said they could keep a cow as well as not, and better too, and Joseph began to believe it. At the suggestion of father G. he borrowed a bag, and on his way home stopped at the grist mill and had it filled with bran, which the old gentleman said was about the best feed for a cow just before coming in. After arriving home "Comfort" received a feed of hay and a quart of bran—had a drink of fresh water, her stable cleaned, some fresh shavings given her for a bedding, and with kind pats and words was left for the night. In the evening bedding was talked over. Joseph thought he would get the privilege of gathering leaves from a wood lot about one half mile distant, but Mary thought they would be too wet at this season, then sawdust was suggested, but that was not quite the thing they concluded, that is, if they could think of anything better. To be perfect it must be comfortable for the cow to stand or lie upon, it must be an absorbent of liquid manure, and something that would add to the value of the compost heap, and would easily decompose. Suddenly Joseph exclaimed, "I have it, just the thing. You remember I went out to N. last fall to do a job of work for Charlie Curtiss's brother, and when he came to bring me home, with my tools, he put a large top box on his wagon box, and also put in a number of sacks. I asked him what he was going to bring home and he said 'oat shucks' to bed his cows with—that the shucks were dry and bulky, and for fifty cents you could get all you could draw at a load. He said it was the best and cheapest bedding he could get, and much more than paid for itself in the value of the manure. That is just what we want, and I will get Charlie to draw me a load to-morrow." So the next night "Comfort" laid down for the first time in her life on a "first-class" bed of oat shucks, while the adjoining stall was filled full for future use.

"Joseph, what are you going to do with that lumber Charlie left here to-day, said Mary," a few evenings later? "Well I have been thinking 'Comfort' ought to have a little yard where she can walk around and enjoy the sunshine and fresh air. I am going to build a fence from the farther corner of the hennery to the fence on the back side of the lot, and one from the corner of the shed back, and that will make her a good yard. Those two English cherry trees will come in it and furnish shade for her in the hottest weather.

Another evening, as Joseph came home from work, Mary asked, "What in the world are you going to do with these," as she drew from the bundle a card and brush. "Which of the family are you going to use these on?"—"Oh, I thought they would be good things to have in the house," said Joseph, laughing. "You know I started out early this morning to go around by Mason's, to see about repairing his house this next summer. He is one of the best of farmers, all his stock look thrifty—everything is up in order, and he makes farming pay. I found him in the stable carding and brushing his cows. That was a new idea to me, and I asked him if he thought it really paid him to spend so much time and labor on his cows. Well, said he, I've had the care of cattle nigh on to thirty years, and I think my carding and brushing pay as well as anything I can do, and there is nothing an animal enjoys more than having its coat combed."

"What did Mr. Mason say about the work."—"He is going to have his house thoroughly repaired, and I am glad to say your husband has the job, and he is going to keep his eyes and ears open and learn what he can about farming."

Joseph had bought a load of fine hay a farmer was taking into town to market, and "Comfort" was now fed hay three times a day, with two quarts of bran night and morning. At noon there was something from the house also, like potato and apple peelings, small potatoes, wilted turnips or beets, cut up cabbage leaves, etc. The children thought it nice fun to feed her at noon. Some loose bars had been put up to her stall which was quite roomy, and she did not have to be driven into it by some of the men and all of the boys in the neighborhood, but when the gate of the yard was opened she walked briskly to her stall, knowing she would find a good supper waiting for her. Humane care, the plenty of food and drink, given regularly, have wrought in a month's time a great change in the appearance of "Comfort." From being a poorly fed "whipped" cow in a dairy, suffering all the discomfort of stanchions for eighteen out of twenty-four hours, with no bed but a bare floor—she has come to be a thrifty, happy animal, giving good promise of rewarding her owners well for their care. One morning the first week in April, Joseph came in from the barn looking pleased, but a little anxious. "Children," he said, "what do you think I found at the barn this morning?"—"Oh, a bossy," they said, delighted with the idea.—"Yes, 'Comfort' has a little 'comfort,' and she is very proud of it; but now comes the rub, who is to milk, and what is to be done with the calf?"—"Oh," said Mary, "I guess I have not quite forgotten how to milk yet, and you can soon learn—'never too old to learn,' you know. I will go out after breakfast and milk out what the calf does not take, and you can go around by Mr. Mason's and ask him what we had better do with the calf." Joseph felt these were good suggestions, and after standing by Mary, in more than one sense, while she performed her part of the programme—which was successfully accomplished—he started for work by way of farmer Mason's. Arriving there he made known his errand. "Well," said Mr. M., "you can 'deacon' it or veal it. Don't many but dairymen follow the first way, and I should advise you to let it have all the milk it wants for four or five weeks, and the butcher will take it and pay you five or six dollars. Put the calf by itself, and night and morning let it go to the cow and get its own milk." When Joseph arrived home that evening, he partitioned off a corner of the barn with some barrels and boxes, put in some bedding, and put the calf in his new quarters. Then he tried his hand at milking, Mary standing by him this time, telling him what to do, and laughing a little at his awkward efforts, yet encouraging him by saying he did splendidly for the first trial. "Comfort" rewarded him for his kindness to her, by being very patient with his awkwardness, and he daily improved in the art of milking, so that while vealy was getting his fill, he would get about two or three quarts as his share.

The latter part of April Joseph commenced work for Mr. Mason, and as his work-bench was at one end of the barn floor, he had a good opportunity for observation. He noticed Mr. M. fed his cows corn meal, and asked him what feed he considered best for cows giving milk at this time of the year. Mr. M. said, in his experience he had found there were three things to be considered in the care of cows. Health of the cow, quantity and quality of the milk. Plenty of wholesome food and pure water (also a little salt each day), given regularly, out of door exercise in pleasant weather, and general good care will give the first. "Clover hay, corn fodder, wheat bran or ground oats, with some roots, will keep up the flow of milk," said he, "but if you want thick cream, and plenty of golden butter, feed your cow corn meal. When my cows are in milk and kept on dry feed, I give each cow daily, morning and evening, four quarts of mixed feed, one part, by weight, of wheat bran and two parts of corn meal, with about one tablespoonful of salt. We make more and better butter on this feed than when the cows have grass only."

Joseph, having no experience of his own, was glad to use that of others in regard to his cow, so from this time he began feeding "Comfort" corn meal, beginning with a pint and increasing gradually to one quart; the result being plainly seen in the improved quality of the milk and condition of the calf When this was five weeks old the butcher took it away giving five dollars for it, and seemed much pleased with his bargain.

That evening Joseph figured a little. He found his bran and corn meal had cost three dollars and fifty-five cents, so there was a balance of one dollar and forty-five cents from the calf to pay on the hay. They had had from three to four quarts of milk per day, of better quality than that they could have bought for six cents a quart. Thirty days, three and one-half quarts a day, at six cents a quart, is six dollars and thirty cents. By stabling and bedding the cow, quite a quantity of good manure had accumulated, and Joseph felt very well satisfied, so far, with his experiment, and most of all for the luxury of having good sweet milk for the family use. It was now the middle of May, grass was well started, and as there were farms near them, it was thought best to hire pasture for the summer. By inquiry they found she could be pastured one-fourth mile from home. This seemed too far to carry the milk, and would take too much time to drive back and forth twice a day. "Why not keep her at home nights, and feed her something as we do now," said Mary; "she will be glad to come home then. Father always feeds his cows bran in the summer; he says it pays in their 'coming up' if in nothing else. He goes to the gate and calls 'come boss,' and they all start as quickly as if he had said, 'come to supper,' and it is that to them." So it was decided to keep "Comfort" home nights. In a few days "Comfort" was introduced to her summer range, and quickly learned the way to and from the pasture, and the children thought it a great pleasure to drive her to and fro.

"Joseph," said Mary, about this time, "what shall we do with the sour milk? The neighbors will take some of it at two cents a quart, but the demand is irregular, and it don't seem right to throw it away. Don't you think we better get a pig?"— "Perhaps so ; as we are in for experiments this year we might try that also. Mason has some nice pigs—two kinds. One kind make large growthy animals, the other kind are smaller but finer, and would be best for us, I think" Soon a pig was added to their farm stock. Joseph declared he would not try to live without a cow again if it cost twice as much to take care of her. "Why we didn't know what good living was until 'Comfort' came to live with us, did we, children?"—"No, indeed, only when we went to grand-pa's."—"Look at this baby," said Mary, "she never was so well before, and she is getting as rosy and round as a Maiden-blush apple. You can't think what a help the milk is to me in cooking. I can always have something fresh and nice now, and it will lessen our meat bill too."

Some of the neighbors wanted to buy milk; "Comfort" was giving sixteen quarts a day. So four neighboring families were supplied each with one quart of milk a day, and after a week's trial Mary reported she had made five pounds of butter that was worth twenty cents per pound, grocery price. They had sold twenty-eight quarts of milk at six cents a quart, butter and milk amounting to two dollars and sixty-eight cents, and they had used all the sweet milk, cream, sour milk and butter-milk they needed, and the pig had been kept on the surplus of the last two. Joseph was now feeding "Comfort" as Mr. Mason advised, with corn meal and bran, two-thirds of the former and one-third of the latter by weight, giving three quarts of the mixture night and morning. Corn meal cost one cent per pound, bran cost two-thirds of a cent a pound, the cost of the feed per day being a fraction over seven cents. He also gave her a little hay—to the value of say ten cents a week—pasture cost twenty-five cents a week, so the expense of her keeping was eighty-five cents a week, the work offsetting the milk used, left a profit of one dollar and eighty-three cents. There was another item not to be overlooked. The manure that was accumulating, the value of which was largely increased by the ground feed given the cow, and the oat shuck bedding. Of the acre of land about one-quarter was occupied with buildings, walks, shrubbery, a small lawn in front, and flower garden at the side of the house, but every foot of intervening space was well seeded to grass, so it really made quite a little mowing. Another quarter had been set out to fruit trees five years, and was now well stocked with red clover, the remaining one-half acre had been used as a garden and potato patch. With the exception of a few loads of manure, obtained at different places, no fertilizer had been used on this acre of land. But now having gone into the stock business, Joseph began to read and think about such things. He frequently brought home an agricultural paper from Mr. Mason's to read in the evening, and began also to feel he must have one of his own. He found considerable in the papers about commercial fertilizers, so he asked Mr. Mason if he had ever used any of them. He said he had experimented with them considerably, and thought them excellent helps. "I have never," said he, "paid out money for anything that came back as quickly with as good profit, as superphosphates. These and other fertilizers must be used with judgment to get the best returns, but on gravelly soil, with a clay subsoil like ours here, it pays well." Joseph also asked Mr. M. what he could raise on his lot to the best advantage for his cow. "I should say sowed corn and mangel wurzels. You see this little lot at the back of the barn, it is ten square rods, and very rich ground."

CORN FODDER.

"I sow this to corn in drills about this time (the last of May), so that it gets well tasseled by the time pastures begin to get rather dry, as they usually do after the middle of summer, then I begin to feed, and it helps keep up the flow of milk amazingly. It is a sweet, juicy and nutritious feed, just the thing for cows. Let me calculate a little. Why Earnest, if your land could be made to produce like this piece, you can raise coarse fodder enough for your cow for six months, on thirty square rods of ground. I like some roots for cows—we like a variety of food, so do animals. The best roots I know of to raise for stock are sugar beets or the mangels."

Very soon after this conversation Joseph had his half acre of land plowed deep and in narrow furrows, as he had seen recommended in agricultural papers. The manure that had accumulated from the cow was used for a top-dressing for one half of the plowed portion. This was well harrowed, and three-fourths of it lightly furrowed with the plow, two and one half feet apart. The remaining one-fourth was turned into ridges as close as the furrows could be turned together. His team work was now done for the present on this part of his lot especially set apart for his cow. (The other half of the plowed lot was to be used for his main family garden, he having spaded up some beds for early vegetables.) He had provided himself with seed corn from farmer Mason's, some mangel wurzel seed from the seed store, and also a bag of two hundred pounds of phosphate, of a brand recommended by Mr. M. The phosphate was sprinkled in the plow marks, at the rate of three hundred pounds to the acre, as near as could be judged, the soil in the bottom of the furrow was lightly stirred with a four pronged potato hook, the corn was sprinkled in, about eight kernels to the foot [sixteen to twenty is better—ED.,] and covered about two inches deep. One half of the piece designed for corn was planted, and the other half left to be treated in the same way some two weeks later. The top was raked off the ridges designed for the mangles. A furrow was made on each with a hand hoe, and phosphate sprinkled in rather more liberally than for the corn. This was thoroughly mixed with the soil, the furrow becoming nearly level with the surface. A line was drawn by which a light mark was made with the end of the hoe handle, in which the mangel seeds were sown and covered about one inch deep, the soil being pressed down lightly with the hoe. After saving enough phosphate for the balance of the corn, and a little to experiment with on some late potatoes, the remainder was sown broadcast on the clover. It fell a little short of covering the whole, and Joseph thought that would make a good opportunity to test its virtues. His seeds came up well, and, as he had all he could attend to nights and mornings, he hired a neighbor to do his farm work, and he determined no weeds should have the benefit of his fertilizers or soil; and this part of his programme was thoroughly carried out during the growing season.

SUMMER QUARTERS.

In "Comfort's" yard was a corner formed by the barn on one side, the hennery on another, and the board fence on a third side. Joseph put a roof over this corner, and about a foot deep of oat shucks on the ground, and fastened a box to the side of the barn for her to eat out of; and here were her summer quarters. Every morning before milking the droppings were cleaned up and piled in one corner of the yard. As soon as the clover began to blossom, an armful was cut each evening and fed to "Comfort" after her ration of dry feed, and the morning feed was discontinued. After the corn was large enough, that took the place of clover until frost threatened; then it was cut up and bound in small bundles, which were set up in large stooks, to cure for winter use.

No difference was observed in the first crop of clover in favor of the phosphate, but the second cutting was largely benefited by its use. Over one-half of the first and second cuttings were cured and stored in the barn, with all of the grass around the yard, which, with fully two-thirds of the stalks, would be nearly, if not quite enough coarse feed to last "Comfort" through the winter. The mangels yielded about twenty-five bushels, not a very large yield, but quite satisfactory, considering the soil had not really been farmed but one year. The roots were pitted near the barn for spring use. Some of the corn stalks were set so as to form a slanting roof over them; three or four inches of dirt thrown over this; afterwards enough to keep them from freezing.

About the first of November, "Comfort" was established in winter quarters in the stall, at night and during stormy days, and in the yard on pleasant days. She continued in milk until the middle of February, and was in fresh milk March eighteenth, was hearty and contented—a comfort to look at as well as to own. Joseph Earnest was well pleased with his year's experiment.

CONCLUSIONS.

It is now three years since he brought comfort to his home in more ways than one. His little farm is improving every year in fertility and value, and even now blossoms like a thing of beauty. Some of his neighbors have followed his example, for he tells them:

"Any one who has a place to put a cow can keep one with profit, if he will make her comfortable; that it matters not whether protection from the weather is secured by logs, straw, sods, rough boards, or planed boards well painted. She must have exercise, sunshine, and fresh air. These can be obtained in a small dry yard, kept clean, as well as in 'Uncle Sam's' pasture, the open prairie. She must have something of a variety of wholesome food, and a plentiful supply of pure water. No domestic animal, in proportion to its weight, needs as much water as a milch cow. She must be kept clean by litter, card, and brush. If these rules are observed with judgment and kindness, very seldom will any help be needed at time of calving. If anything goes wrong there is no better rule than to use one's common sense, taking the advice of experienced neighbors.

"To economize manure, an abundance of good litter should be used, and the compost heap kept under cover, if possible; at any rate, not under the eaves of the barn. If, with this home-made manure, your land does not produce all it can, and you wish to buy some fertilizing material, your first choice should be good stable manure; if you cannot get that reasonably, use some reliable brand of commercial fertilizer. Have your cow 'come in' when it will be most for your profit or convenience, avoiding hot weather. The calf may be killed when one to three days old, saving its hide and rennet; it may be kept until five or six weeks old, fed on new milk, and 'vealed,' or sold for that purpose, or it may be raised on skim-milk (after it is three or four weeks old), and sold in the fall to some farmer.

"Milking should be done gently but quickly, as near twelve

hours apart as possible. Milk clean but do not "strip;" use the whole hand, and not the thumb and finger only; sing or whistle, if you want to while milking; if you are good friends with your cow, she will enjoy it.

"Since the first year I have not bought any coarse feed, and only a little fertilizer for grass and clover, the cow and pig furnishing all that is needed for the plowed ground, and this last year I have a surplus of feed. I tell you, friends, my cow is the best savings bank I ever knew."

This and much more said Joseph Earnest to his neighbors.

A GOOD STABLE "TIE."

Mr. D. C. Kenyon, of Carbondale, Pa., describes a convenient home-made Stable Tie as follows: Our tie, of which we send you a miniature sample, is made of three-eighths inch rope, which is braided into an iron ring sliding freely up and down a post set close to the manger or feed-box. There is a knot or frog on one end, and a loop on the other. The ends pass on each side of the cow's neck, and the knot is slipped through the loop which may be made tighter by twisting. Similar fastenings made of chains with snap-hooks may be bought at the hardware stores, but such an one as is here described will last a long time and answer every purpose.

Fig. 15.

JERUSALEM ARTICHOKES AS COW-FEED.

BY CHRISTOPHER SHEARER, TUCKERTON, PA.

Butter and milk are not only luxuries, but in many families they are indispensable necessaries of life. In this article my principal purpose is to show how a cow can be kept with the greatest economy of land and labor. I consider these the essential points in the discussion. Where hay is dear and pasture scarce, a man who lives by the labor of his hands, cannot ordinarily afford to purchase the necessary food for a cow; and if he has only an acre or two of land at his disposal, he finds it more profitable to raise other products. Ordinarily it requires the yield of several acres of land to support a cow. But I propose to show that this can be done on less than one acre, by raising the proper crops, and treating the soil to the best advantage. A cow of ordinary size will consume about eleven thousand pounds of hay, or its equivalent, in a year. The equivalent of this amount of hay is—in potatoes, thirty thousand eight hundred pounds, or five hundred and thirteen bushels, and in Indian corn, seven thousand seven hundred pounds, or one hundred and thirty-seven bushels. These quantities cannot be raised on one acre, and if we examine the tables of equivalents of food, we find that most of the grasses, grains, and roots, are objectionable on account of unproductiveness, want of sufficient nutritive qualities, or of the labor that the cultivation of them requires.

VALUE OF ARTICHOKES.

There is, however, a root, or tuber, an acre of which affords enough nourishment to sustain two cows, with less labor than is employed in raising an acre of potatoes—and that root is the Jerusalem Artichoke (*Helianthus tuberosus*). We can depend upon an average yield of from one thousand to one thousand two hundred bushels of these tubers from an acre of land rich enough to produce fifty bushels of corn. Pound for pound they are equal in nutritive qualities to potatoes. One cow can therefore be subsisted a year on five hundred or six hundred bushels of the tubers, a quantity that can be raised on half an acre of land. But since these roots do not keep over summer, and as the cow will not thrive on them alone, it is necessary to supplement them with dry fodder during winter, and to subsist her on other forage during summer. With the aid of this plant, three-quarters of an acre of land under high cultivation, will nourish a cow during the whole year, and the soil will become rich without any other manure than that derived from the cow. This can be done with little expense, and with no more labor than is involved in ordinary farm culture. It is necessary to begin operations on the farm in most sections of the Middle States, a little earlier than the first of May.

A cow can be subsisted to the best advantage on a small patch of land, by feeding her Jerusalem Artichokes and a little hay or other dry fodder through the winter and part of spring, and soiling her with green rye, clover, and green-corn fodder, the rest of the year. Three-quarters of an acre will, under judicious treatment, yield enough of these products to maintain a cow during the year. If the soil be not in good condition to begin with, that quantity of land may, for a year or two, be insufficient for the purpose, and it will then be necessary to supply the deficiency from other sources; but by proper management the land will, in a few years, be converted into a garden that will afford abundant nourishment for the cow, without pasture or outside aid either in food or manure.

Suppose that a man owns a cow of medium size, or a little larger, that he has three-quarters of an acre of land, that one-third of it, namely, one-quarter of an acre, is in clover, that the remainder is ready for the plow, and that it is early spring-time of the year, he should go to work at once and manure the land liberally, for he will be well repaid for the expense, in the superior productiveness of the soil. All the land, excepting the clover, should be plowed, and one-sixth of the land, that is one-eighth of an acre, should be sowed with oats, with about one-half bushel of seed. One quart of clover seed, and one pint of timothy seed should be sown on the oats. The oats are raised only during the first year, rye being substituted in after years, and the timothy is added for the purpose of increasing the hay-crop in the second year. One-third of the land (one-quarter of an acre) should be planted in Jerusalem Artichokes, early in the season. This root should be planted in hills, three feet apart each way, and cultivated flat, both ways. As the land increases in fertility in future years, the hills may be set a little farther apart. The patch should be stirred two or three times with the cultivator while the plants are young, and afterwards kept clear of weeds with the hoe. The weeds require but little attention after the plant has attained a fair growth. One tuber, or piece of tuber, of about the size of a hen's egg, is sufficient for a hill, the seed being covered to the depth of two or three inches with earth.

As soon as the season is far enough advanced, one-sixth of the plot (one-eighth of an acre) should be planted in sweet corn. One half of the corn should be set out very early, and the rest about four weeks later, so as to extend its growth, and consequently its availability as green fodder, over a longer period. The furrows should be three feet apart, and the corn planted in drills, [sixteen to twenty kernels to the foot—ED.] Afterwards the corn should be cultivated two or three times, and kept clear of weeds. When the corn fodder is all disposed of, the corn patch should be plowed, and seeded with about a peck of rye, and a pint of timothy seed, and in the following spring a quart of clover seed should be sown upon the rye. These crops will give the land a complete rotation every six years. The following diagram indicates the proper succession of the crops and shows the plot of land divided into six equal parts, containing one-eighth of an acre each:

1st Year.	2nd Year.	3rd Year.	4th Year.	5th Year.	6th Year.
Clover.	Artichokes.	Artichokes.	Corn.	Rye.	Clover.
Oats.	Clover.		Artichokes.	Corn.	Rye.
Corn.	Rye.	Clover.		Artichokes.	Corn.
Artichokes.	Corn.	Rye.	Clover.	Clover.	Artichokes.
	Artichokes.	Corn.	Rye.		Clover.

Clover occupies two parts, rye one part, and Jerusalem Artichokes two parts every year. Clover follows rye; rye follows corn; corn follows artichokes; and artichokes follow clover. Every year one-half of the clover, namely, the two-year-old clover patch, is plowed, and planted in artichokes. The latter must be planted anew, and not be allowed to grow as a "volunteer crop," but must be regularly cultivated, and all the plants that come up between the hills destroyed.

The manure derived from the cow during the winter, should be spread in spring on the land intended for corn and artichokes, and plowed down, and that made in summer should be applied to the rye and clover patches in fall. Ashes and a moderate quantity of lime, spread on the clover patch early in spring, will be beneficial, and a peck of gypsum scattered on the young and growing clover, will answer an excellent purpose as a healthy stimulant of its growth.

The spring-time of the first year must be tided over with hay until the clover is large enough for soiling. Green clover is then

Fig. 16.—SWISS COW "GENEVA."

fed to the cow until the oats are sufficiently advanced. The oats are then used as long as they are fit for the purpose, cutting them a second time as far as practicable, and the residue, if any, is cured for hay before it gets too ripe for that purpose. The same course is pursued with the rye in the following years. The clover should be cut for hay rather early, in order to get it in the best possible condition, and to insure a good second, and perhaps a third crop. All the aftermath not used in soiling, should be converted into hay. When the oats are exhausted, clover is fed until the corn fodder is large enough for use. This is fed until the ears make their appearance, and what is then left is cut and cured for dry fodder during winter. After the green corn fodder is all consumed, there will be a growth of new clover in the oats stubble the first year, and in the rye stubble in after years, with which the cow is soiled until the artichokes are ready to feed, and if any of the new clover is left by that time, it is made into hay. The artichokes are fed raw; in winter, with hay and other dry fodder, and as long as they last in spring.

In the second year soiling begins with rye, and continues afterwards through the season the same as the first year, and a like course is followed in succeeding years.

FEEDING ARTICHOKES.

The artichokes will grow until frost kills the stalks, and a patch of one-quarter of an acre, when the soil is in good condition, will yield a yearly average of between two hundred and fifty and three hundred bushels of them. They can be fed before they are quite ripe, in which case the cow will eat up the whole plant—root, stalk, and branch. She must not have access to a heap of the tubers, lest she surfeit and seriously injure herself. As long as the whole plant is fed, she should not be allowed more at a time than she will eat up clean, for if she gets more she will eat the tubers, and refuse the stalks. In fact she will prefer these tubers at all times to any other food. She should therefore receive a certain allowance, say a peck or a little more, three times a day, so that she will eat up the stalks, and also a small portion of other forage with them. In winter and spring she will consume a bushel or more of the raw tubers a day, together with eight or ten pounds of hay or other dry food. Her ration of artichokes should never be so large that she will reject other food.

Artichokes can be fed for about eight months of the year, say from the first of October to the first of June, during which time the cow will consume two hundred and forty bushels, or more, of them. These, with the hay and other dry fodder, will keep her in excellent condition, and produce an abundance of good milk without additional food. One ton of hay or other dry fodder, in connection with the artichokes, will last during the said eight months, affording the cow eight or nine pounds a day. Three-quarters of a ton may suffice, but she should not have less than this. If the crop of hay and other dry fodder exceeds a ton, it may all be fed during the first year, or a part of it may be kept over for the ensuing year. In stowing away the hay, ten or twelve quarts of salt should be scattered through a ton of it, to impart a relish. In addition to this, the cow should receive two or three ounces of salt daily, and plenty of pure fresh water.

HARVESTING ARTICHOKES.

The artichokes should remain in the ground in autumn as long as the weather permits, and be fed out of the field during that time, and just before the earth is permanently frost-bound, enough of them should be dug up to last over winter; and, since frost does not injure them, the rest should be left in the ground until the following spring. A good way to keep them in winter, is to place them on the ground in the field in shallow layers, covering them lightly with the stalks of the artichoke, or with straw, and then with a little earth. If the rain wets them it will not injure them. It is advisable always to keep a considerable quantity of them in the stable or cellar for convenience of feeding. In the ensuing spring, they are again fed out of the field until it is time to plow the land, when all the tubers not yet disposed of, are taken up and kept in the cellar or stable.

THE STALKS

of the Jerusalem Artichoke furnish excellent material for litter for the cow. They grow to a hight of from eight to ten feet, are composed almost entirely of pith, and are so fragile that they can easily be broken into fragments. As many of them should be stowed in the stable as it will contain, and the rest, if any, should be stacked outside. Before bedding the cow with them, it is advisable to crush them with a mallet on a block prepared for the purpose. This labor will require but a few minutes daily to provide sufficient litter, and will make a comfortable bed for the cow, absorbing and retaining the liquid manure. The stalks cannot be used for fodder after being frost-killed.

If the food of the cow should at any time run short the deficiency must be supplied, for it will not do to stint her, and if it is ever found necessary to change or modify her diet, it should be done.

I have allowed three-quarters of an acre for the sustenance of the cow, and this will be sufficient, but only on condition that the land is in good heart. If the land is poor at the start, it will be safer to begin with more, and afterwards to reduce the quantity to three-quarters of an acre, as the soil increases in fertility. The value of clover as a renovator of the soil is well known, but the Jerusalem Artichoke is equally efficacious, if fed on the farm, for it attracts its nitrogen to a great extent from the atmosphere. The dairy-farm now under discussion possesses all the advantages that can be derived from these plants as fertilizers, and as the other crops raised on it do not injuriously exhaust the soil, being cut before they produce their seed, the land will improve indefinitely in fertility.

THE CALF AND THE CARE OF IT.

Since the plants here recommended for the nourishment of the cow, afford the best milk-producing food the whole year round, the time of calving may be left to the option of the owner, for it will not affect the quantity of milk that the cow gives. If the milk is mostly needed in summer, the cow should calve in spring, and if it be desirable to have more milk in winter, she should calve in autumn. I might add, that if the butter, or a part of it, is to be sold, it will be more profitable to have the calf in fall than in any other season, because butter brings the highest prices in winter.

The disposal of the calf depends on circumstances, of which the owner is the best judge. If he concludes to keep it on account of the value of the breed, or for any other reason, he should raise it by hand, not allowing it to suck more than three days at furthest. For the first few days it should receive only the fresh milk of the cow; afterwards it may be fed on warm fresh milk, skim-milk, buttermilk, whey, and hay-tea, until it is old enough to subsist on solid food. Fresh milk should be the leading diet in the beginning, and should be gradually diminished in quantity as the calf increases in strength. Hay-tea is made by pouring boiling water on hay, and letting it steep for about two hours. If the calf is not to be raised, it ought to be sold before it is a week old, because the milk that it drinks before it is ready for the shambles, is worth more than the price it will bring. If a purchaser for the calf cannot be found while it is so young, it is most profitable to kill it, and bury it in the compost heap, as soon as the milk of the cow is fit to use. I simply state this as a fact, without recommending it to be done, for it is cruel work; but so is any butchering, and if the calf is to be killed, it really matters not how soon it is done. The sooner it is removed from the cow the less she will grieve for its loss.

CALVING.

The cow should be milked as long as her milk is good, or until she runs dry, which may in some cases be six or eight weeks of calving (in others not at all.) Her rations should be curtailed a little for a short time before that period, in order to carry her safely through the crisis. After she has the calf, she may receive warm bran-mashes for a day or two, containing a little of her own milk, and should not be fully fed for the first few days. This treatment is all that is required before and after the period of calving. The cow will generally pass through this event in safety, without assistance. Should there, however, be a false presentation, or other difficulty of parturition, the best thing the owner can do, if he has no experience in the matter, is to call to his aid a veterinary surgeon, or a neighbor who knows what course to pursue in such cases.

As long as the cow is fresh, and yields a large flow of milk, she should be milked three times a day, early in the morning, at noon, and late in the evening; afterwards two milkings daily, will be sufficient. She should be fed, watered, milked, carded, and led out of and into the stable, at the same hours every day. She should not be beaten, or pelted, or harshly spoken to or dealt with in any manner. Kind and considerate treatment inspires her with confidence and contentment, makes her the pet and delight of the household, and is rewarded by an abundance of wholesome milk. But there are many matters of detail in keeping a cow, which it is impossible to notice in a limited essay like this. If the owner desires to be fully informed on the subject, he will do well to purchase a few books that treat upon the subject.

The stable for the cow should be warm, dry, well ventilated, and large enough to contain two or three tons of hay and litter, together with other material to be described hereafter, besides a stall for the cow, and room for the calf. If the owner of the cow has a stable that fulfils these requirements, it will answer his purpose if he makes a proper stall in it. If he has no stable, and cannot afford the expense of building a good one, he must at least have a proper stall to save the manure of the cow, and to shelter her from the inclemency of the weather. A stable that will fully answer this purpose, should be at least fourteen feet square, and about twelve feet high to the eaves, and should have a loft for storing hay. The annexed figures represent such a structure in outline:

Figure 17 is a ground plan, and shows that the lower story is divided into two parts, *S*, representing the stall, and *R*, all the remaining portion below. The stall is ten feet long, and should be five, or nearly five feet wide; *M*, represents the manger, which is about two feet deep, eighteen inches wide, and in length equal

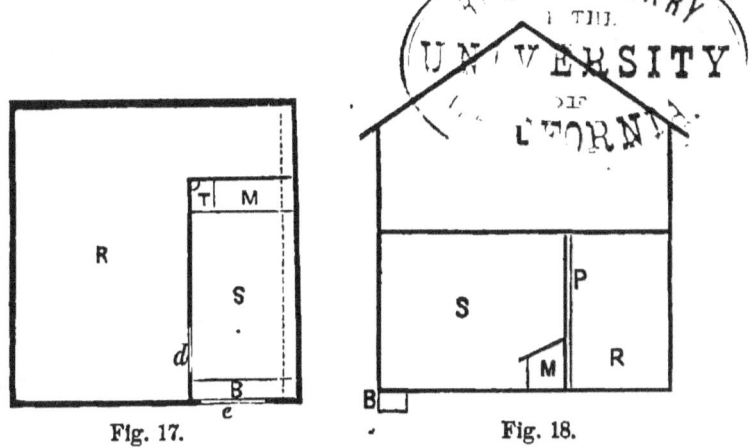

Fig. 17.   Fig. 18.

to the width of the stall. The cow is tied to the manger with a halter or chain; *T*, is a trough in the manger for feeding roots, salt, etc., and is about one foot wide, eight inches deep, and in length equal to the width of the manger. The floor of the stall should slope a little to the rear, and must be water-tight, so as to conduct the urine of the cow into the brine-pit, *B*. The floor may be composed of cement, or of two-inch plank closely fitted together. The brine-pit, *B*, consists of a water-tight box made of plank, and should be about one foot wide, six inches deep, and in length equal to the width of the stall. This pit is sunk into the ground so that its top is on a level with the floor, in order that it may receive all the liquid discharges of the cow that are not absorbed by the litter. If the floor is laid in cement the pit may be made of the same material. The object of the brine-pit is to save the liquid manure; to accomplish which the latter must be retained by some absorbent.

4

Dry earth is used for this purpose. At first the bottom of the pit is covered with dry earth, and as soon as this is moist, more earth is added until the pit is full of the saturated substance, when the latter is thrown upon the compost heap, and the same process repeated. A door is placed at *e*, for admitting the cow, and carrying away the manure. The partition between *S* and *R* may be made of boards or rails, and need not be over four feet high.

The division, *R*, is used for keeping litter, dry earth, artichoke roots, green fodder, and the calf. It should have a door at some convenient place for entrance from the outside, and a window with a glass-frame, preferably on the south side. It is in communication with the stall by means of a gate at *d*.

Figure 18 is a view of the gable-end, *L*, representing the loft for storing hay and other dry fodder. The loft has a shutter in one of the gable-ends or sides, and a ladder or steps running up to it from within, for convenience of feeding. *P*, is a post in the corner of the manger. The other letters in figure 18 indicate the same parts as in figure 17.

The cow-yard will be large enough if it contains an area of two square rods; but it can be made somewhat larger with advantage. It ought to adjoin the stable so as to give the cow direct access to the stall; and ought to be shaded by trees in order to afford shelter to the cow from the direct rays of the sun in summer. The cow should be kept in the yard only a part of the day, and the rest of the time she should be in the stall. The stall-door should be left open when she is in the yard, so that she can enter the stable at will. Some manure will be lost by suffering her to run in the yard; but the benefit that she will derive from it, in health and contentment, will more than compensate for the loss.

MAKING AND SAVING MANURE.

The compost heap may be kept in the cow-yard, and must be in the shade. It should, therefore, be placed on the north side of the stable, and trees should be planted east and west of it. It must not be under cover nor washed by running water, nor receive the water from the roof of the stable; but the rain should fall on it directly from the skies to promote decomposition, and to prevent the escape of its volatile constituents. The manure of the stall, and the saturated earth of the brine-pit, are mixed together to form the compost heap, and all the refuse material of the farm, garden, and yard, should be thrown on it. It ought to be kept in a compact body, level on top, and protected by boards on the sides to prevent it from spreading. No ashes or lime should ever be applied to it.

Regarding the material for absorbing the liquid excretions of the cow, nothing better can be found than prepared muck; but as this is seldom obtainable, the scrapings of the streets of a city, or even of a public road, may be used instead. If these cannot be had, the surface soil of the dairy farm answer the purpose. Whatever substance is employed must be thoroughly dried. The middle of summer is the proper time to prepare it. About four cart loads of it, as dry as they can be made, should be kept in the stable, or in some other place where it is not liable to attract moisture; and that amount will last the year round.

CONCLUSIONS ABOUT ARTICHOKES.

I have now given my instructions for keeping a cow, and it is evident from what I have written, that the Jerusalem Artichoke is my main dependence for her support. The other points that I have touched upon, are of minor importance, when compared with the value that I have attached to this plant. My own experience with the plant satisfies me that I have not overstated its merits. On rich land a single stalk will produce from a peck to half a bushel of the tubers. Last year was an exceptionably unfavorable one in this locality, on account of drouth in summer and fall; and yet the artichokes that I planted between the trees in my peach orchard yielded abundantly. I have fattened cattle on them without any additional food excepting a little hay, until they were fit for the butcher; and my horses thrive on them when fed in connection with hay, doing full work without grain. A brother of mine planted artichokes in a field that had been in cultivation for more than a century, and yet in spite of the drouth, of indifferent culture without manure, and of an early frost that prematurely killed the plants, the yield amounted to between five hundred and six hundred bushels to the acre.

RURAL ECONOMY.

Boussingault in his "Rural Economy," pp. 159-160 says: "The Jerusalem Artichoke rises to a hight of from nine to ten feet; it flowers late, and I have not yet seen it ripen its seeds. It is propagated by the tubers which it produces, and which are regarded, for good reason, a most excellent food for cattle. * * There are few plants more hardy and so little nice about the soil as the Jerusalem Artichoke; it succeeds everywhere with the single condition that the ground be not wet. * * Of all the plants that engage the husbandman, the Jerusalem Artichoke is that which produces the most at the least expense of manure and manual labor. Kade states that a square patch of Jerusalem Artichokes in a garden was still in full productive vigor at the end of thirty-three years, throwing out stems from seven to ten feet in length, although for a very long time the plant had neither received any care or any manure. I could quote many examples of the great reproductive power of the Helianthus; I can affirm, nevertheless, that in order to obtain abundant crops, it is necessary to afford a little manure. * * Schwertz estimates the mean quantity of dry leaves and stems at three tons, one cwt., one quarter and fifteen pounds per acre."

Again, p. 401—"Experiment with horses.—Jerusalem potatoes are held excellent food for the horse; they are eaten greedily, and he thrives on them. In this second experiment 30.8 pounds of Jerusalems cut into slices were substituted for eleven pounds of hay, the same theoretical equivalents being assumed for them as for the common potato. The ration now consisted of hay, eleven pounds; straw, five and a half pounds; oats, seven and a half pounds, and Jerusalem potatoes, 30.8 pounds. Having been accustomed to this regimen for some days, the teams were weighed, and having gone on for eleven days, they were weighed again:

	Team No. 1.	No. 2.	Both Teams.	Mean per horse.
In eleven days,	gain 55	loss 33	gain 22	gain .9

"A result which leads to the conclusion that the equivalent assumed for the Jerusalem potato was correct; the animals had done their work, and gained one with another nine-tenths of a pound in weight."

Again, p. 406.—"One hundred pounds of good meadow-hay may be taken, as ascertained by experiment, to be equivalent to

280 of Potatoes,	by analysis equal to	315
280 of Jerusalems,	" "	311
400 of Beets,	" "	548
400 of Swedes (too little),	" "	676
400 of Carrots	" "	382

Again, p. 415.—"One thousand parts (by weight) of the forage gathered at Bechelbroun in its ordinary state contained:

	Mineral Substances.	Azote.	Phos. Acid.	Lime.	Bone Earth.
Potatoes,	9.61	3.70	1.09	.17	.33
Beet,	7.70	2.10	.46	.54	.95
Turnip.	5.70	1.30	.35	.62	.72
Jerusalems,	12.47	3.75	1.35	.29	.53

Again, p. 449.—"Seventh experiment—with a cow two hundred and ninety days after calving.—In this trial the ration consisted of Jerusalem potatoes equivalent to thirty-three pounds of hay, under which the milk may be said to have remained stationary, though it was above rather than under the six pints per diem, as in the sixth experiment," (with Irish potatoes).

I consider, therefore, that, according to experiment and analysis, the Jerusalem Artichoke is fully equal to the potato as food for stock, and greatly superior to beets, turnips, and carrots. In the regimen that I have prescribed for the cow, I have given the Jerusalem Artichoke the preference over all other roots, because I deem it superior to them in all respects. It contains more nutriment than any of them, excepting the potato; it is less exhaustive of the soil, and more efficacious in improving it; it produces a larger crop; it is less liable to failure in adverse weather; it keeps better and with less care: it is eaten with a greater relish by stock; and it requires less labor in cultivating, harvesting, and feeding it. Analysis has shown that it contains its carbonaceous principles in the form of sugar instead of starch, 14.8 parts of uncrystallizable sugar having been found in one hundred parts of the tuber. It has no starch cells to be broken up by boiling, in order to make it a digestible aliment; and how large soever the tubers may be, they can be fed without being cut into slices, on account of their fragility and brittleness, being masticated by the cow without difficulty or danger of choking.

The Jerusalem Artichoke is little known and cultivated in this country, and its merits are not fully appreciated anywhere. The reason probably is because there is but a limited demand for it in the market. But it should not be neglected on that account; for it is not the less valuable, because the profits derived from it are indirect. It should never be raised as a volunteer crop, as is too often the case, but should be regularly planted and worked like other products. I have discussed this plant as advantageous food for "one" cow, and I may add that it is equally meritorious for any number of cows. But its advantages do not stop here. Horses, cattle, sheep, and swine, thrive and fatten on it, and the millions of acres of exhausted and deteriorated lands, that descend as a profitless inheritance from generation to generation in the Eastern and Southern States, can be improved and kept fertile, with profit to the farmer during the process of renovation, without the aid of artificial fertilizers or imported manures, by feeding the tubers of the Jerusalem Artichoke to stock on the farm.

VIEWS AND PRACTICE OF A PRACTICAL FARMER.

BY F. E. GOTT, SPENCERPORT, N. Y.

Having been a practical farmer all my life, with considerable experience in the care of stock and dairying, I give you the result of my experience. The system of management which would be profitably adopted by one would be utterly impracticable for another. In my own case I have about one acre of land, one half of which I set apart for production of food for my cow, while the remainder is occupied by the buildings in part, and the rest is devoted to the culture of small fruits. Without this land I should be obliged to hire my cow pastured through the summer, at a cost of about fifty cents per week, which I am now able to save by practising a system of soiling. The advantages of which are numerous.

PROFIT IN BUYING PART OF THE FEED.

I am aware that the amount of land which I have devoted to this purpose is inadequate. One acre would be none too much to supply a cow with food through the year, but I can realize more profit by purchasing a portion of the necessary food and devoting part of my land to the culture of small fruits, the amount of money received from the sales of which, will more than pay for the feed that I could raise on the same land.

My barn (figs. 19 and 20) is inexpensive, yet it answers every purpose. It consists of a box-pen for the cow, an open shed and a pig-sty, the whole covered by one roof, and occupying a space twenty feet in length by fourteen feet in breadth. It is constructed of hemlock lumber. The posts on the front are twelve feet in hight, while those on the back side are eight. It is boarded vertically and battened on the sides, and the roof is also covered with rough boards, laid on double, breaking joints so that no water can leak through. The box for the cow is eight feet by ten, and is six feet and four inches high in the clear. Adjoining this is a feeding passage four feet by eight. The arrangement of doors is shown in the accompanying sketch. The middle portion of the building is an open shed, and is seven feet wide by fourteen feet long. It is used principally for storing dry muck and also as a cover for the manure pile. Adjoining the open shed is the pig-pen. While the partition between the cow-stall and shed is carried up to the floor above, making a tight box stall, that between the pig-sty and shed is only built four feet from the ground, leaving the upper part open. A floor is laid at a hight of six feet ten inches from the ground, which provides storage room for hay above. I would

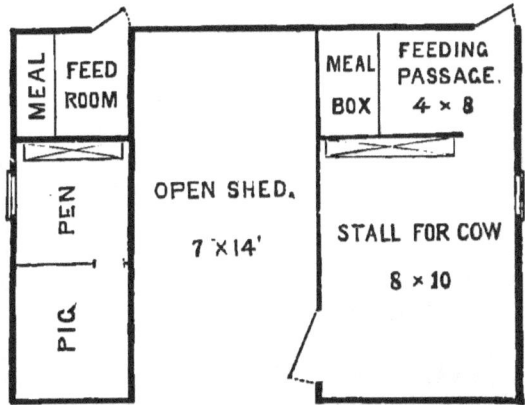

Fig. 19.—PLAN OF COW-SHED, ETC.

suggest, as an improvement to this plan, that the whole be built two feet higher, making the long posts fourteen feet instead of twelve, and the short ones ten instead of eight, thereby securing more room above. There would then be sufficient room for the

Fig. 20.—PERSPECTIVE VIEW.

storage of over two thousand pounds of clover hay. Of course the provision I have made for a pig is outside of the question under consideration, but in view of the fact that wherever a cow is kept, a pig may also be profitably raised and fattened on the skim-milk and much that would otherwise be wasted, and at the same time increase greatly the value of the manure heap, I think such provision should be made, especially as the cost of such an addition to the cow's shed is but little. In case it is not desirable to keep a pig, the space may be used as a calf-pen or for the storage of straw. The cost of the building which I have described should not exceed fifty dollars.

The only way to secure a good cow, is to keep trying until we get such a cow as we want and then hold on to her. We may have to change several times before we can bring this about, but there is no infallible rule for selecting a good cow. Were I to select one for myself, I should select one not over five years old, of gentle, quiet disposition, with a large barrel; one whose udder is large and well formed, with teats set well apart, of good size, and projecting slightly outward from each other, and with large milk veins.

The method which I have adopted in the management of my cow, has this in its favor, that it has been highly and uniformly profitable to me.

MANAGING THE MANURE PILE.

I shall first present my mode of making manure, and of applying the same. The prevalent idea among those who keep a single cow or other domestic animal is, that the manure, instead of being saved and protected from loss with the greatest care, is a nuisance, which should be summarily disposed of. It is an established fact that the liquid portion of the excrement nearly, if not quite, equals in value the solid portion, and in order to save both we must provide some means by which the liquid and volatile portions of the manure may be prevented from going to waste. This is best accomplished by means of absorbents, and there is nothing better or cheaper for this purpose than dried muck or earth, a good supply of which should be constantly kept under cover where it is easily accessible. Fortunately I am so situated that I can obtain a supply quite easily. There is within half a mile from my place a large tract of swamp land, from which I can obtain, for a low price, all the "muck" I need. Every fall, I store away under my shed a sufficient quantity to last me through the winter. This had previously been thrown into piles and dried. It is quite essential that it should be thoroughly dried, so that it will readily absorb the liquid manure, and this may be accomplished by piling and allowing it to be exposed to sun and air for six months or a year before wanted for use. The bottom of the stall is covered with ten or twelve inches of the dry muck, over which I scatter a light covering of cut straw or sawdust, so as to secure a clean bed, and prevent the particles of dirt and muck from sticking to the cow and dropping from thence into the pail. The dry earth readily absorbs the liquid droppings and whenever it becomes saturated with the same, may be removed, together with the manure and soiled straw, to a pile beneath the covered shed, when a fresh supply of dry muck, enough to replace that which was removed is carried in and the whole is again covered with the cut straw. An occasional sprinkling of plaster (gypsum) is applied both to the litter in the stall and to the manure heap, which prevents any loss of ammonia, and hence all unpleasant odors are avoided. Whenever a forkful of manure is put on the pile, it is immediately covered with muck. Twice each year this is hauled on to the land. Manure thus treated will not waste, either by the leaching out of soluble matter, by the escape of ammonia, or by fire-fanging. And as there is no coarse material, such as long straw or corn stalks mingled with it, it is always in a suitable condition to use. If dry earth or muck cannot be obtained, cut straw or sawdust may be substituted. But earth, being an excellent deodorizer itself, and containing, as it does, much valuable fertilizing matter, is much to be preferred.

If artificial fertilizers are used, they may at any time be mixed with the compost heap. Also, when a pig is kept, its pen should be cleaned daily and the litter, mingled with the general pile, will add greatly to its value. Common salt may occasionally be added to the compost heap with advantage, but ashes never, as they tend to liberate the ammonia and thereby cause waste.

YARD ROOM AND EXERCISE.

It is not necessary to have a large yard connected with the stable, as a cow is seldom inclined to exercise her locomotive powers more than is required to secure her food, and if this is placed before her at suitable times and in sufficient quantity to supply her demands, she will remain perfectly contented in an enclosure twenty feet square. In planning our buildings let us bear in mind that sunlight is essential to perfect health. Therefore we should have the yard on the sunny side of the building. At the same time we should see that there is a shady corner, where the cow may take herself during intense heat. A hint in this direction is sufficient. Nothing can be more cruel than to force any dumb animal to stand exposed to the rays of an August mid-day sun, or where she is tormented nearly to death by flies. Yet we often see just such inhuman neglect on the part of those who should know better.

Although in many respects desirable, a pasture lot is not absolutely essential, and in the case of the villager, whose land is measured by feet instead of acres, it must be dispensed with. Hence we have recourse to what is termed the soiling system, which is simply cultivating such crops as will produce a succession of green food throughout the season, and placing the same before the cow in such quantities and at such times as she may require, instead of allowing her to tramp around after her feed, and thereby waste more than she eats. It requires some skill and judgment to carry out this plan successfully, but wherever it has been practised judiciously and intelligently, the results have been uniformly satisfactory. As to what amount of land is required in order to keep a cow through the year, I will not pretend to say; nor do I think it advisable to try to produce the entire amount of food required for a full year's sustenance.

HAY.

I know that for me it is far better to purchase what hay will be needed to feed through the winter than to attempt to grow it. Besides, our village lots are much too small to be profitably converted into hay fields, and even if there should be more land than is necessary to furnish the soiling crops for summer feeding, it is usually much better economy to employ the same in the cultivation of small fruits, which, as I have before stated, more than pays for what hay is required, besides supplying us with many luxuries.

In my own case, I have set apart one-half of an acre from which to supply the cow with food during a period extending from May first to November first. Now this will be entirely insufficient, except under the very best cultivation and management, which, of course, I am bound to bestow upon it. That it is sufficient, with proper care, I have repeatedly proved. Such results could hardly be expected, however, from land which has received no previous preparation, and is worn, wormy, and weedy. Let us assume, then, that our half acre is in a good, fair state of productiveness. To produce a continuous supply of wholesome fodder, I find a system of rotation must be practised, and have subdivided my half acre into four equal parts, containing each one-eighth of an acre, or

KEEPING ONE COW.

twenty square rods. These I shall designate as plots one, two, three, and four. Plot one is at the present time in clover, having been seeded one year ago, and will be ready for use about June. Plot two was sown to winter rye last October, and will be seeded down with clover this spring. From this patch of rye I shall obtain the earliest feed, and will begin using it about May first. Plot three will be sown with corn, drilled thickly in rows two and a half feet apart, which, if sown as soon as danger from frost is past, will be ready for use about August first. Plot four will be sown to mangels or sugar beets. I prefer the latter, and this is the only crop cultivated for winter use. Both this crop and the corn are planted with a garden seed drill, while the rye is sown broadcast. On the first of May I begin cutting the rye. Up to this time the cow has been fed on clover hay, and grain.

I calculate to have the cow drop her calf at about April first. To this end I have her served about June twenty-fifth. Of course, we cannot always have our own way in this matter, but, accident excepted, we can usually manage so as to approximate the time. During a period of a few days subsequent to parturition, I feed quite sparingly—however, allowing her all the long hay she will eat, together with a peck of beets twice a day, but no grain of any kind, this reduced ration being necessary to avoid the danger which might result from the too abundant secretion of milk at this time, which high feeding would tend to produce. If at the end of the fifth day after calving, no bad results have occurred, such as milk fever, and there is little or no caking of the bag, I begin to gradually increase the feed, until, at the tenth day, I reach the normal standard, which is as follows:

DAILY FEEDING.

At half-past five A. M. I feed her four quarts of a mixture consisting of one part each of corn meal and oat meal, and two parts of bran. Four quarts of this is mixed with a heaping half bushel of cut (chaffed) hay, moistened but not soaked. While she is occupied in eating, I clean the manure from the stable, remove all dirt from her udder, and any that would be likely to drop into the pail while milking. Sometimes a sponge and water are required to accomplish this, but usually an old piece of a blanket kept for the purpose is all that is necessary. I then milk and carry the milk directly to the house before it has time to cool or absorb odors, which, even with the utmost care and cleanliness cannot be entirely avoided. After breakfast, I give the cow a peck of sliced beets, on which has been sprinkled about a dessert spoonful of salt, which completes her breakfast. At this time it is a very good plan to use the curry comb or card for ten or fifteen minutes, though I must confess that I sometimes neglect this part of the programme: still I think that my cow gets far more indulgence in this direction than most cows in the neighborhood. After she has finished eating, if the weather is not too unfavorable, I allow her to run out in the yard, where, at noon, I give her just as much long hay as she will eat up clean, and no more.

There is at all times plenty of fresh water in the yard, to which she can help herself whenever she so desires; otherwise she would need to have it supplied to her at least twice a day, but not immediately before or after a feed of grain. At half-past five in the afternoon she receives the same amount of food, and prepared in the same manner as in the morning. This method is continued until the crop of rye is large enough for use. All changes from dry to green feed must be made gradually, if we would avoid loss. By this time our supply of roots will be exhausted, but the green food, in a measure, takes the place of them. I continue to give the same amount of grain throughout the summer as I did through the month of April, and also to mix it with chaffed hay slightly moistened, as this insures the complete mastication and thorough intermingling with the saliva, which is so essential to perfect digestion and assimilation. As the supply of green food increases, I diminish the quantity of chaffed hay until but one-half the former amount is used, which quantity is continued through the soiling season. The one-eighth acre of rye will last until about June fifteenth, at which time the red clover will be large enough to feed. We should not change abruptly from one kind of green food to another, but increase the one and diminish the other gradually until the change is complete. To ascertain the exact amount needed for a feed of this kind, as well as of the other green crops, requires some judgment on the part of the feeder; but a very safe rule is to feed just such an amount as the cow will eat clean, and no more. We cannot specify exactly what would be a proper amount in every case, neither can we spend time to weigh each ration, but, by observing carefully, we are enabled to determine very closely. I find that my cow will eat, besides her other feed, a good armful of green fodder three times a day. I always cut a day's supply on the afternoon preceding, and allow it to remain in the swath, where it will wilt, and a portion of the water evaporate, thereby rendering it more

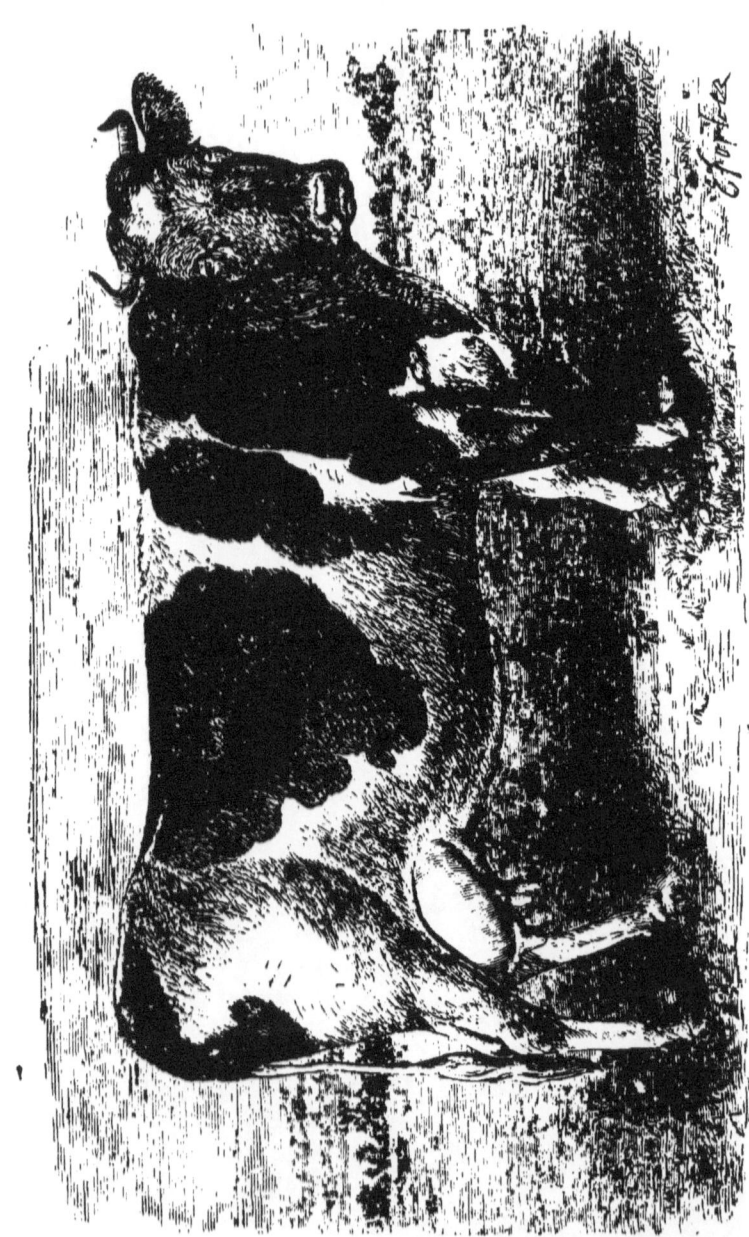

Fig. 21.—THE DUTCH (HOLSTEIN) COW "CROWN PRINCESS."

wholesome than when fed immediately after cutting, and I think my cow relishes it better. By the fifteenth or twentieth of July the clover will have become so ripe as to necessitate the cutting and curing of any that may be left at that time. It may still be fed, however, for a few days, or until the sowed corn becomes large enough to take its place, which is generally about the first of August. This crop, and the second cutting of the clover, will complete the course, and will furnish feed until well along into October, or the first of November, after which I depend on purchased food.

WINTER FEED AND TREATMENT.

If not previously done, I now procure three thousand pounds of the best early cut clover hay. As my shed is not sufficiently large to store away this amount, I am obliged to stack part of it. I also procure bran and meal. The amount of these which I require for a year's supply is: of bran, one thousand pounds; of corn meal, one thousand pounds; and of oat meal, seven hundred and fifty pounds. These amounts, well mixed together, will furnish a feed of eight quarts per day, which amount is diminished during the period in which the cow is dry, and is sometimes increased, if by any means other food is short. It is not advisable to procure all this feed at once, for, if stored, it would be quite likely to heat and mould before it could be used, besides being subject to loss from rats and other vermin. I therefore procure one-sixth of this amount, or two months' supply at a time, and I have often found it convenient and profitable to buy the corn and oats and have them ground myself. The course pursued in feeding from November first until February fifteenth, at which time the cow becomes dry, is similar to that which I have described for the month of April. It is better to dry off the cow four, five, or even six weeks prior to calving. Sometimes, in order to do this, it will be necessary to omit the grain and diminish the quantity of roots for a few days, but after she becomes quite dry I resume feeding as before, except perhaps to lessen the amount of grain until within a few days of calving, when I omit the grain entirely until, as I have before stated, the danger from milk fever, etc., is past.

CALVING.

Some people continue to milk their cows until within a very short time of calving. This is very poor economy. The milk at such times is thin and insipid, and unfit for food. I have never found any "preparatory treatment" of the cow prior to parturition, such as physicing, etc., to be necessary; but place her on short rations for a few days—administering, as one writer terms it, "judicious starvation." The feed of roots is continued, as they exert a laxative effect on the bowels and tissues, thereby obviating the necessity of giving a huge dose of Epsom Salts. In an experience of fifteen years, by following this plan of restricting the diet, I have not had a case of milk fever, apoplexy, or retention of placenta, and but one case which called for assistance, and this was due wholly to an accident. When a single cow is kept, she is, of course, exempt from the ill consequences which so often result from crowding and fighting with other cows, and, if kindly treated and provided with comfortable accommodations for feeding and shelter, she will seldom have any trouble. But cases where assistance is indispensable do sometimes occur, even under the best management, the most frequent of which is the retention of the placenta or after-birth. If, at the end of twenty-four hours, the cow has not "cleaned," it is then time to undertake the removal of the placenta. This can be accomplished by carefully introducing the right arm of a man having a small hand, which should previously be well greased, into the cavity of the uterus, when the connecting attachments will readily be found and may be separated, after which the whole may be brought away. These attachments are often quite numerous, and care should be taken that all are detached, and that the whole of the after-birth is removed, as serious results sometimes occur when a portion of it is retained.

If, from any cause, the fœtus has got into an unnatural position, or shows any other presentation than that of the two fore feet and muzzle, natural labor may be rendered impossible, and assistance will be required in order to set matters right. There are several abnormal positions in which the calf may be presented, while there are but two positions in which delivery is practicable. In the natural position the two fore feet and nose are the parts which make their first appearance. When this is the case we may generally conclude that our services will not be required. If, on the other hand, there is any alteration of this position, either by the absence of the head or of one or both feet, or if, when labor pains have continued for some time, there is no presentation at all, it will be necessary to investigate the cause. The owner's duty, in cases of this nature, will be to restore it, by judicious manipulation, to its normal position, or to such a position as will render delivery practicable. If, from the nature of the case, the fore legs and nose of the fœtus cannot be brought into such a position, we must endeavor to bring up the hind legs and deliver it in that position. It frequently occurs in this position, as well as sometimes in the natural one, that traction will have to be applied. In such cases it should be applied simultaneously with the throes of the cow. In rare cases it becomes necessary to amputate portions of the fœtus and bring them away separately, which operation should be left to the veterinary surgeon. In fact, whenever assistance is required, it is better to employ the services of a competent surgeon, if such can be obtained. But where professional assistance cannot be obtained, it is much better to use one's own judgment than to depend on the village cow doctor, who is usually one of the most ignorant persons in the community. Happily, cases requiring any assistance, where a single cow is kept, are rare.

For *Mamitis* or garget I have given successfully the following powder twice daily: Pulverized Digitalis, one drahm; Nitre, one ounce; Cream of Tartar, one-half ounce; mix and give in the feed. If the bag is caked and hard, let the calf run with the cow for a few days.

I do not consider it profitable to raise the calf, therefore I dispose of it as soon as possible. There are always plenty of farmers or farmers' boys who are glad to buy a good calf to raise, and will willingly pay one or two dollars for the same, and take it right away. I prefer to raise and fatten a pig instead.

ACCIDENTS AND FAILURES.

It is no more than fair for me to say concerning my plan of feeding, that I have occasionally been obliged to modify some of the details, on account of unfavorable circumstances. For instance, I have been forced to cut grass from the highway in front of my house, to supply a deficiency in some crop, caused by unfavorable weather, or some accident or other. In the spring of 1878, my clover failed to catch, leaving me to make up for the loss of that crop as well as I could. It was certainly most unfortunate, inasmuch as it seriously interfered with the whole system of rotation. To carry out the plan of soiling successfully requires considerable time and labor. And on the whole, unless one has plenty of the former at his disposal, and a good wholesome inclination for the latter, he could do full as well to adopt the old time practice of having his cow pastured by the week, in which case no other labor than milking would be required, while, if she were allowed a feed of meal or bran at the time of milking, night and morning, very satisfactory results would be obtained.

ONE YEAR'S RESULTS.

To show what I have accomplished by it, I will give an account of the products of my cow "Polly," for the year ending April first, 1880, together with a statement of the actual expenses of her keeping. Besides what was used in a family of four, I have sold one hundred and sixty-nine pounds of butter, at an average of twenty cents per pound, which amounts to thirty-three dollars and eighty cents; eight hundred and twenty-eight quarts of milk, at six cents per quart, forty-nine dollars and sixty-eight cents; eighteen quarts of butter-milk, at three cents per quart, fifty-four cents; eleven quarts of sour milk, at two cents, twenty-two cents; one calf, four days old, one dollar and seventy-five cents; total, eighty-five dollars and ninety-nine cents. To this I may add one hundred and twenty pounds of butter consumed at home, twenty-four dollars, and about two hundred and thirty quarts of milk, worth thirteen dollars and eighty cents; making in all, one hundred and twenty-three dollars and seventy-nine cents. The cost of feed was as follows: One thousand pounds bran, nine dollars and sixty cents; one thousand pounds corn meal, eleven dollars and fifty cents; seven hundred and fifty pounds of oatmeal, nine dollars and eighty five cents; three thousand pounds clover hay, thirteen dollars and fifty-cents; two hundred pounds rye straw, one dollar and fifty cents; muck, two dollars; total, forty-seven dollars and ninety-five cents; leaving a balance of seventy-five dollars and eighty-four cents. As I keep a horse, I have the necessary tools for cultivating the land myself, I have not added the cost of cultivation as an item in the expense column, and perhaps it may be said that I should also have added interest on land and buildings. As an offset to these, I would call attention to the valuable pile of manure, and furthermore I have made no account of a large amount of skim-milk, on which I raised a pig. This pig was fed nothing but sour milk, and a very few small potatoes, until about four weeks prior to butchering, when he was "finished off" on corn meal. He weighed, after being dressed, December twenty-eighth, two hundred and seventy-eight pounds. The profits from this cow would undoubtedly have been larger had I sold all the milk, instead of making butter out of a part of it, but I did not make mere profit my sole object in the matter. I wished to supply my family with those necessary luxuries which, I believe, are rendered even sweeter by the consciousness of their being the products of our own labor. The pleasure which I have taken in caring for my pet cow, and in providing for her wants, and the pride I feel in exhibiting both my cow and the delicious rich milk and yellow butter, with which she so bountifully supplies us, amply repays me for my part of the labor. I have made no account of using concentrated food, such as oil-cake and cotton-seed meal, for the reason that I have had very little experience in the use of them. Whenever an animal has become thin and poor, these articles of food may be used to advantage to increase the flesh and bring the animal into good condition. But I never let my cow get poor, and I find that good hay, with corn, oats, and bran, answers every purpose, and is fully adequate to all her requirements. My system of rotation is as follows: The one-eighth acre of clover sod of the preceding year is well manured either during the winter or in the spring, and well fitted up and sown to beets or n angels. This crop occupies the land during the whole season. The same plot is again plowed the next spring for sowed corn. After this crop is off it is again manured and sown to rye, and the following spring is again seeded to clover. It is kept in clover one year, yielding two crops during the season, after which it is treated as before. Each of the four plots undergoes the same treatment; thus a complete rotation is established.

KEEPING A COW ON CAPE COD.

BY M. T. T. NICKERSON, SOUTH DENNIS, MASS.

We live in a section of country where nature has not been lavish with her gifts. Our soil is sandy and only produces paying crops by high cultivation. Farming with us comes near to being one of the lost arts. We are not tillers of the soil. Living, as we do, within sound of the Atlantic surf, as it beats its everlasting measure upon our coast, we, from associations of birth and early training, plow the Ocean for a living, the furrows frequently stretching from pole to pole, or to the opposite side of the globe. Few, very few, keep cows. A large proportion of our people do not keep any, and it is not common to find many that have more than one.

We keep a good grade Jersey, and will give our way of keeping one cow, having learned long ago, that stock of any kind paid for good care. Keeping a lot of cattle or hogs, or poultry, and simply feeding what we happen to have, or what we can buy cheap, leaving them to shift for themselves in cold and stormy weather, or giving them wet uncomfortable stables, always results in disease to the stock and loss to the owner.

We sow as early in the spring as the ground is in condition to work, forty rods with a mixture of oats and peas, and forty rods in spring rye. We commence cutting our oats and peas as soon as the peas begin to bloom. Where we have a good stand, a rod per day, divided in three feeds, morning, noon, and night, is generally enough. As soon as we have cut about ten rods we plow under the stubble, and plant Early Minnesota Sweet Corn—rows two and one half feet apart—hills two feet in the rows, leaving two and three stalks in a hill. The next ten rods we serve in the same manner. If our rye is now grown enough to cut with profit we commence feeding it, and cut the balance of our oats and peas, and cure them for winter.

If our rye is not fit to cut for soiling, we continue to use our oats and peas until it is, and then cure for winter what is left. As soon as the last of our oats are off, we plant about four rods with beets (mangel wurzel). We prefer the Globe varieties, as the yield is better on our soil. The balance of our oat-and-pea ground we sow with Hungarian grass.

As soon as we have cut ten rods of our rye, we manage as with our oats, turn under the stubble and again plant sweet corn. The earlier the variety the better. We prefer the Early Minnesota. As soon as we have cleared off the next ten rods of our rye, we plant from two to four rods with turnips. The balance we sow with a mixture of Hungarian and the earliest "Canada Gray" pea. We now feed our rye until our first planting of corn and Hungarian will do to feed, when we turn under the rest of the rye stubble (curing what is left of the rye for winter), sow half with Hungarian and the balance we sow (not plant) with sweet corn. As soon as our first planting of corn is cut up, we sow two or three rows broadcast with flat turnips, some of the strap-leaved varieties, hoeing or raking them in by hand. We continue to plant or sow some quick-growing variety of corn, peas, grass, grain, or roots, even when it is very doubtful if we shall receive any return for our time and work; but we frequently get a fair yield from our third planting. I presume a great many will be sceptical in regard to this "third crop business." It must be remembered that our first sowing is made very early in the spring, and that we do not wait until any of our forage crops mature, but we cut them long before they would be ripe, thereby shortening the time of their growth and leaving the ground to be planted with something else.

The above is no iron rule, but subject to great variations. Our plan is to sow as early as possible in the spring with the earliest maturing grass or grain we can get, and from the time we commence cutting until there is no possibility of getting any return. We sow and plant wherever we have a few rods of bare ground, as soon as any of our crops are maturing or there is something coming forward to take its place. We cut and cure what is left for winter. We advise close seeding in all cases, roots, of course, excepted.

COW KEPT ON HALF AN ACRE.

If the season is favorable, we manage to keep our one cow nicely on half an acre, or rather on the fodder grown on half an acre. But sometimes, on account of drouth or late frost, we are obliged to buy a little hay in the spring.

It is impossible for us to say how much feed must be bought. We generally have a bag of corn (two bushels), and a bag of oats (two and a half bushels), ground together, feeding from two to four quarts a day, according to the amount of roots used, and the season of the year, feeding meal very sparingly in summer. We frequently reserve two or three rods in the spring for early turnips, to be fed when large enough for profit, but always feed turnips immediately after milking to prevent flavoring the milk. We generally have a few cabbage plants started to set where the corn misses, or the beets or turnips fail to come up, or in any corner or by-place where there is room for a cabbage to grow. Sometimes we reserve a few rods for cabbages late in the season, as we find them excellent for a change of feed either winter or summer. We advise, in all cases, the use of the earliest varieties of grass, grain, or vegetables, as we cannot afford the time and ground occupied by some of the larger and taller growing varieties, being convinced, from actual experience, that two and three crops of early varieties, although small, are more profitable than one crop of the larger late varieties.

THE STABLE AND THE MANURE CELLAR.

The stable for our cow is a shed nine by sixteen, built on the south side of our carriage and wagon house. One-half of the shed is partitioned off and enclosed for winter use or stormy weather; the other half of the shed is open on the south side, and our yard is about sixteen by thirty, including the shed. We think it would be better to have it larger, but we get along with it nicely. We find the best way to dispose of her manure is to have a small cellar underneath the stable, with cemented bottom and sides, so as to be water tight, the stable to have a tight floor with a gutter behind the cow to receive the droppings and urine, with a scuttle or trap door in the gutter to let it all go into the cellar. For bedding, we use forest leaves, and use them liberally. Where forest leaves cannot be obtained, any refuse hay or straw will answer, but the cow as well as the horse should have plenty of good dry bedding. To mix with the urine and droppings of the cow, we put into the cellar, sea-weed, muck, turf, slops from the house, and soap suds, or anything we think will make good compost. We gather up the droppings from the yard and throw them into the cellar. We keep our yard well laid with forest leaves. If those are not available, we use the next best thing we can get. In the fall, when we cart the manure out of the cellar, we gather up what has accumulated in the yard and put it into the cellar. In this way we save all of the manure, and in excellent condition. Now, to make it better and save the labor of pitching it over, we keep a pig where he can have access to the cellar, and if not disposed to work, we keep him on short feed and scatter corn in the cellar, so that in order to get it, he will have to root the whole mass over in good shape.

We cart our manure out in the fall, distributing it over our land as evenly as possible, and plow it under as deep as we can. We do not sow anything for next year's use, as we think we get a better return from our land to sow early in the spring and continue it through the summer. It is a mistaken idea, or rather a grave blunder, to undertake to grow good crops of anything without the liberal use of manures. As soon as our land will do to work in the spring, we sow our oats, peas, and rye, giving a top dressing of guano, superphosphates, or bone meal, which we repeat with each successive sowing, also giving each hill of corn and rows of beets and turnips a small quantity. We alternate the top dressings, that is, if we use superphosphate the first sowing, we use ground bone or guano the second, and vice versa, as we find the continuous use of any one kind of manure or fertilizer is as injurious as continuous planting of corn or potatoes, without rotating with something else.

BARRELS FOR KEEPING ROOTS.

We have a way of our own for keeping our roots in the absence of a vegetable cellar, or when we do not want them in the house cellar. We take any old barrels and set them in the ground, the chiner just coming to the top of the ground (we do not want a head in either end of the barrels). Into these headless barrels we put our beets, turnips, cabbage, etc. As the weather grows cold we cover the barrels with some loose boards. Whenever it is cold enough to freeze hard, we throw over them enough hay or straw to keep out the wet. By this method we can, with very little trouble at any time, get out a barrel or part of a barrel of roots. In this way the roots keep in fine condition. Late in the spring, turnips and beets will be as brittle and good as when pulled in the fall. Our subject is "keeping one cow," but any one that feels disposed to try it, will find the above a very fine way to keep turnips, beets, cabbage, or celery, for family use.

We prefer to have our cow calve about the first of April, as we then have time to make veal of the calf before we begin to make grass butter. There is generally, in any place, a better demand for milk through the winter, and better prices, hence if one wishes to sell milk and buy butter, it would perhaps be better to have her calve in the fall.

We hardly feel competent to advise, if help is needed in calving. As her time of calving draws nigh, we give our cow extra care and attention. If the bowels are kept in a healthy condition, we apprehend there is rarely trouble, from the fact that our cows have always calved without the need of help.

If there is ready sale for milk at paying prices, we would dispose of the calf in some way, when it is a few days old, but if milk is not salable at good prices, it is better to let the calf have the milk until from four to six weeks old, and then if the butcher will not give us a fair price for it, we get some one to dress it for us, and sell it among our neighbors, who are generally glad to buy it. In that way we get from eight to twelve dollars for our calf. We think it as well for the cow to keep the calf for that length of time. It seems to satisfy a necessity of her nature to have her baby suck and draw its nourishment from her. We know of no better picture of contentment than to see an old cow suckling her calf after being away from it all day.

We advise regular hours of milking night and morning, and kind, gentle treatment, carding in winter, cleanliness and thorough ventilation of stable at all times. In summer time, if confined in a yard, a thin sheet to keep off the flies will be found very comfortable for the cow, and profitable to the owner. I presume some will ridicule the idea of blanketing the cow, but why not as well as the horse? Again, if confined in a yard, she should have plenty of clean pure water, and plenty of shade. Keeping a cow, with us, is not altogether a matter of fancy or pleasure, but of convenience, economy, comfort, profit, and health, in having pure sweet milk and fresh butter.

ALFALFA OR LUCERN.

BY SAM'L C. HAMMER, DOWNEY CITY, CAL.

I have lived in Tennessee, in Texas, and now reside in California. I have been using Alfalfa for some eight or ten years, and from my own personal care of and attention to this article, I maintain one can obtain more milk the year round from it, without change to other food, than from any one thing grown. Besides, Alfalfa can be grown at less expense, and is attended with less labor, whether fed green or cured, than any other feed.

Alfalfa can be grown in Canada, it is said. If so, then any one has the chance to try this wonderful friend to the farmer. Once sown on deeply cultivated land, free of weeds, it is good for ten years, or even more, with us. Twenty pounds is abundant seed for an acre—some think too much; but it should be sown thickly. Let it stand thick, and it is finer and more tender. Where sown sparsely it becomes woody and coarse. It can be cut here as early as March, where mowing and not grazing is adhered to, and it should never be grazed or "staked" (fed off by tethered cattle). From seven to nine cuttings can be obtained from it, and from fifteen to twenty tons of cured hay a year made to the acre; that is, if on good land and if the crop fully occupies the ground, and is cut just as a few scattering blooms are observed. This hay must be cured as rapidly as possible, raked in windrows and bunched the second day, rather letting it cure in bunches than in any other manner, to prevent leaves falling off; then housing or "shedding" it soon as possible, sprinkling salt through it as stacked, to prevent mould.

Alfalfa needs no top-dressing with fertilizers and manure, but simply a severe cross-harrowing with a very sharp-toothed harrow, bearing the weight of a man. The more the Alfalfa is torn and split up the better it will grow. This harrowing should be done in spring before it commences its first growth. After growing a few years, the stools project, in many places, above the surface of the ground. If an implement could be devised for the purpose of cutting off all these old stalks just below the surface, then seed lightly, giving a good harrowing, the plants would be renewed, and would thicken up rapidly, for wherever a stalk or root is cut off, dozens of new shoots spring up in its place.

However, I advocate a change of diet for brutes as well as mankind, and therefore take for the family cow a half acre of most excellent ground. I will suppose that one half of it—that is a quarter acre—is well set in Alfalfa. The rest I would have plowed twice, very deep, smoothed and laid off in drills for carrots, which, at the proper season (with us in February or March), I would enrich in the furrows with any well-rotted manure. For Alfalfa almost any good soil suits, for I find it adapts itself to various soils and endures a great deal of rough treatment, but in order to get the best results it should be well treated. I prefer a moderately sandy soil, which is naturally moist. On dry, mellow ground, it will send down a tap-root ten feet. I have drawn roots out of very sandy soil when digging post holes that would measure six feet. They seek moisture during dry weather, and although I have had Alfalfa die down, the ground being parched and cracked, yet when the fall or winter rains begin, it springs up in a few days.

As soon as the Alfalfa comes in, feed it alone, salting as suits one's own idea. When the first scattering blooms appear I would cut the remainder—namely, that which had not been cut each day for the cow. I would then cure it as rapidly as possible, and put it under cover, sprinkling salt over it. I now advocate and practice feeding the cured hay in preference to the green. By the latter you obtain a greater flow of milk, but with the former I consider the milk richer, and this is the experience of dairymen with whom I have conversed.

A cow learns to eat the cured fodder almost as readily as the green, and all danger of bloat is obviated. Some may think because I am in California that irrigation makes some difference, but my Alfalfa grows without it. I cut mine six times last summer, 1879, and it was an exceptionally dry and hot season. Our rains fall mostly in winter, and that has to do us until the next winter.

Now, as to the cow, I would place her in a corral or lot, we'll say, of one-fourth to half an acre in size, giving her a comfortable house or shed for winter, in which I think she should be fastened by a closed door in cold rainy weather. At other times she should be allowed the run of the lot, having access to good fresh water at least twice a day. Shade trees for summer's hot sun are indispensable. In this lot or corral you have all the manure where it can be gathered up daily or weekly, and composted or housed, ready to be spread on the ground for future crops. Some would say a cow should be curried every morning. They certainly do enjoy it, but many California farmers never saw such a thing done. I think it should be done just before the animals begin to shed their old coats; afterwards I see little use of it.

PERMANENT GRASS AS SOILING CROP.
BY P. S. NORRIS, ANGELICA, N. Y.

The keeping of one cow seems to be generally regarded as a matter of so little importance, and one so simple in its nature, that even persons of low intelligence can scarcely fail of success. But to keep a cow in such a manner as to receive the greatest return for the least possible expense in labor and money, requires the most careful study of the nature and habits, endurance, needs, and the productive capabilities of the animal, and involves scientific principles which are deeper and broader than those generally applied to the keeping of stock of any kind.

If the average quantity of milk be ten quarts per day during the year, and the expense twenty cents per day, the milk will cost two cents per quart, and if the milk is worth three cents per quart, there is a net profit of fifty per cent upon the cost of keeping, or ten cents per day. But if the quantity of milk be eight quarts per day, and the expense twelve cents, the milk will cost only one and a half cents per quart, or twelve cents per day. Then three cents per quart for the milk will leave an actual profit of one hundred per cent upon the cost of keeping, or twelve cents per day.

One acre, and even something less, put in good condition, well fertilized and properly seeded, will be ample for a pasture, and will furnish plenty of nutritious feed, upon which, with proper care, the cow will yield an abundant flow of rich and delicious milk; while one-third of an acre of similar soil will produce sufficient hay for the winter. The pasture should be divided into two parts, the cow to be kept a few days in each alternately, with plenty of pure water and shade. Where land is high, as it always is in towns and villages of any size, the practice of "soiling," as it is usually termed, is the most profitable way to keep a cow. For this purpose, a small yard, some twenty to thirty feet square, perhaps, or of such size as can be afforded, may be provided, containing an open shed—the more open the better for the summer—only so that it will shelter the animal from the heat of the sun and the storms. The yard and shed should be kept as clean and dry as possible, or the cow will become ill. Plenty of pure water is indispensable at all times. A comfortable place for the cow to lie down is very important. Sawdust, forest leaves, old straw, or other convenient and cheap litter will answer for bedding; or, if the ground be smooth, clean and dry, that may be sufficient. The manure is to be carefully collected and placed under another shed, or other convenient place under shelter provided for the purpose, and, to prevent bad odors, the heap should receive, once in two or three days, a light covering of muck, leaves, sods, weeds dug up in the garden or elsewhere, or fine earth—almost anything that will rot—and thus not only prevent the unpleasantness and unhealthfulness of such odors, and the loss that would result from their escape, but add largely to the size and value of the manure heap. Now, have about two-thirds of an acre of land, highly manured, and, with the exception of about fourteen square rods, well seeded with a variety of nutritious grasses. This quantity of land, if properly enriched and cultivated, will keep a cow the year round, and keep her well, without purchasing any feed. A good rack or other arrangement in the shade is necessary, in which to feed, so that nothing shall be wasted. Then, quite early in the season, the grass upon this rich soil will be large enough to be cut and fed to the cow. While the ground is sufficiently moist, in the fore part of the season, the grass will grow very rapidly, and, when the soil becomes a little too dry, about half a bushel of plaster, or twice as much lime, or two or three bushels of wood ashes, scattered upon it, will usually renew the vigor and freshness of the crop, which may be repeated with benefit two or three times before the end of the growing season. Another excellent fertilizer, which may be applied during the summer, is the waste water from the house, such as soap suds, dish water, and any other slops that are to be thrown away. These should all be saved and scattered upon the grass from pails, if no better method is ordinarily practicable, and it will pay a person many times over for the trouble. A light top-dressing of manure from the cow-yard or shed will be necessary every year, or every second year certainly, applied in the fall, or early in the spring.

As soon as the grass has fairly got into blossom, it should be immediately cut and well-cured for winter use, unless it may be necessary to save a small quantity to feed until that portion which was first cut for the cow shall be ready to cut again. Grass should never be allowed to stand until the seed has formed, as just previous to that time it is more nutritious than at any other period. Hay cut thus early will make much more and better milk, and keep a cow in better condition than that which is cut later. A portion of the grass can be mown a second time for hay, and still leave enough for green feed until foddering time. The exact proportion of the crop to be made into hay must, of course, depend

Fig. 22.—SHORTHORN COW "COLD CREAM."

upon circumstances. All that is not needed for summer use should be cured for winter, and the quantity will, generally, be sufficient, if, indeed, there is not an overplus, as will quite likely occur in many cases.

BEST KINDS OF GRASSES.

It is important to know what kinds of grasses are best adapted to the production of milk and butter, for both summer and winter feeding; and upon this depends, in a great measure, the profits to be realized. The practice of seeding with a single kind of grass, or even with a mixture of clover and timothy, is not a good one. Four of the most nutritious and productive kinds of grass, including timothy, white clover, and such other varieties as are well adapted to the particular nature and condition of the soil, are none too many to be sown together, for pasture or meadow. Five quarts of timothy, three of white clover, six of orchard grass, and three of red-top (if the ground is quite moist), or other grass suited to the soil, are about the proper quantities and proportions for general use, on an acre of land. Such a mixture, upon a rich soil, will produce fully twice as much feed as any one kind upon the same soil. White clover produces a greater quantity and better quality of milk and butter than any of the other varieties of grass, and the quantity of feed produced by such a mixture, will astonish any person not acquainted with the facts. Besides producing much more abundantly, they furnish something of a variety of feed, which is greatly beneficial in the manufacture of both milk and flesh. Weeds injure the flavor of milk and butter, and should never be in the food for cows. An acre of rich soil, well seeded with a good selection and variety of perennial grasses, will produce six tons of well-cured hay in one season; by mowing twice, and, by early cutting, this can be done without difficulty. In my own experience, the first mowing has given at the rate of full four tons per acre, and the second, somewhat injured by drouth, two tons. Some writers recommend the sowing of one or more of the rank growing annuals, as being more productive; but a careful consideration of the subject, accompanied by experiments, discloses the fact that the extra expense of preparing the ground and seeding annually, overbalances any increased quantity of feed produced, especially when the coarser and less nutritious nature of the feed is taken into the account. There is nothing suited to this climate and latitude, that will answer a better purpose as food for stock, than such perennials as timothy, red-top, orchard-grass, blue-grass, the clovers, etc., when sown upon a rich soil, thick enough to completely cover the ground and to insure fine, soft hay, when cut at the proper time and well cured. I have omitted red clover in the mixture of grasses, because soils adapted to that variety will produce white clover equally as well, and in about the same quantity, while the white gives a much better flavor to milk and butter, and an increased quantity. Blue-grass, either green or cured, is excellent feed for cattle, but is unprofitable on account of the small product, and that coming only in the fore part of the season, failing, as it does, just at the time when fresh feed is most needed. Red and white clover may be advantageously mixed with the true grasses, in many localities where the soil is suitable, though the clovers are likely to "run out" in a couple of years, and leave their places to be filled with inferior fodder plants.

MILKING THREE TIMES A DAY.

During the heat of summer, the cow should be milked three times a day, at regular intervals—about five o'clock in the morning, one in the afternoon, and at nine in the evening. The quantity of milk and butter is considerably increased, and the quality improved, by this practice. The milk is injured by remaining in the udder through the heat of the day, and the cow is made uncomfortable, which, of necessity, diminishes her usefulness. When cows are milked but twice a day in hot weather, the udder becomes too much heated and feverish, and the milk is in a similar condition—the cream seems to be melted, the milk soon becomes sour, the cream does not rise well, and the butter is soft and oily. These difficulties, almost universally attending butter-making at this time of the year, are mostly overcome by the practice of milking three times a day, and the cow being near at hand, it is a small matter.

The length of time a cow should be milked, will depend on her capabilities for giving milk a longer or shorter time. Some will give milk the year round, while others will "go dry" three or four months, or longer, in spite of all efforts to keep them in milk a longer period. But, as a rule, it is better for a cow to go dry some eight weeks, giving time for fleshing up a little, and gaining strength for another season. The cow will be more vigorous, and the flow of milk more abundant afterward.

THE ELLSWORTH OR "BARRE" SYSTEM OF FEEDING.

BY D. D. SLADE, CHESTNUT HILL, MASS.

My own experience, as well as that of others, has taught me that a cow properly fed twice a day, will give more milk, and be in better condition than when when fed three times, or more frequently. This plan, which is known as the "Barre" system of feeding, may be adopted throughout the year, although it has been chiefly applied to the winter months, in the region where it has been most extensively pursued.

The poorest quality of fodder is given first, at the commencement of each meal, and before this is entirely consumed, another foddering of a better quality is placed before the cow, and finally a third, of the best hay. After this is consumed, roots, grain, etc., may be given immediately. In this way, the animal employs on an average about two hours at a meal—which occurs only twice during the day, with an interval of from six to seven hours between the morning and evening. Water, always slightly warmed, in cold weather, is offered at once, and it will be found that the cow will not drink so freely after she has begun to chew the cud. No food should be given between the meals, which should be at regular hours, and served with punctuality. So long as she chews her cud, which in the well-fed cow is about six hours, we can rest assured that her digestive organs have work enough before them, and that we cannot reasonably call upon them to do more.

The why and the wherefore of this system of feeding, which we heartily advocate, are well told in the words of Mr. Ellsworth, the originator. "The idea that a cow needs only two meals a day during the winter season, as long as she is kept upon hay or other dried fodder, notwithstanding the fact that she will eat much oftener, when obtaining her living from the pasture, may appear to the casual observer, to be contradictory to itself; but on a closer investigation we shall notice a rational, and I believe satisfactory reason for it. Of all the elements of which grass is composed, by far the larger part is water, which must render it much more bulky than an equal amount of hay, and for this reason, more is required to supply the wants of the system. During the season, therefore, when the cow must live by her own exertions, she must labor most of the time to obtain the requisite amount of nourishment, which she is not required to do while in the barn. We must not forget, also, that pastures in general are kept down so close during the greater part of the summer, that only by continual labor can her wants be satisfied."

The same rules are applicable to the soiling of the cow during the summer months, the only difference being that green food is given in the place of dry. This may consist of rye, oats, barley, millet, or Hungarian grass, corn, English grass, etc., cut while in the milk. It will frequently be found that a proportion of dried hay will also at times be highly relished, and may be essential to allay any excessive looseness of the bowels, which may be produced by the succulent food.

During the time of eating, the milking and other necessary work may be done about the cow house, so that time may be thus economized.

As to the requisite amount of food, it may be taken as a safe rule, that a milch cow demands in food, three per cent of her weight. An average cow, then, will require from eighteen to twenty pounds of hay, in addition to a peck or two of roots per day, or the equivalent of this amount in green food during the summer months.

If the hay is good, and has been properly cured, or if rowen can be given, then there will be little or no demand for grain in any form. If otherwise, from one to two quarts of Indian meal, with two quarts of shorts per day, should be fed out, if we are to expect a good flow of milk. We have found excellent results to follow the practice of stirring the meal and shorts, or a portion of these, into a bucket of warm water, and offering this mixture immediately after the animal has consumed her dry food, and before any roots are eaten. This extra amount of fluid will be greedily taken, in this way, without any interference with a liberal supply of water at the end of the meal. Salt, at all times, should be accessible to the cow, and perhaps this article may be best supplied by placing a large lump of rock salt in the manger, to be licked as her wants may require.

Taking Central New England, as before remarked, as the latitude of experimentation, it will be found that one square rod of oats, Hungarian grass, barley, rye, and similar grasses, in proper condition, growing on land in a high state of cultivation, is amply sufficient for a cow for one day. Or in other words, to be within perfectly safe bounds, and considering the chances of partial failure, we may say, that under the conditions above mentioned, forty square rods, or one quarter of an acre, will produce ample food for one cow for thirty-five days. On this basis, upon one acre can be grown soiling material sufficient to keep a cow through the year, allowing also, a liberal amount of roots. How is this to be done?

We may assume that a man takes possession of a place on the first of April, which is the customary time in New England. Let him select an acre of the land most suitable to the purpose in view. Let him set apart forty square rods, or one quarter of it, for summer soiling, twenty square rods for the growth of roots, and the remaining one hundred square rods for crops, to be properly cured for winter use. The land having been thoroughly prepared, that is, in high tilth, sow as early in April as possible, on ten square rods, oats, or spring rye, at the rate of four bushels to the acre. This will be fit to cut, for summer soiling, in the first week of July.

On the fifteenth to twentieth of April, sow the next ten rods in a similar manner. This will be ready to cut about the fifteenth of July. On the first of May, sow oats or barley on the next ten rods, which will be fit for cropping August first.

On the tenth to the fifteenth of May put in the next five rods in drills, flat corn at the rate of three bushels to the acre, and a week later the remaining five rods are to be treated in a similar manner. This will give succulent food up to September.

As soon as the first ten rods of land, which were cleared of oats by the tenth of July, has been again prepared properly, sow Hungarian grass at the same rate as before stated. Do the same also with the next lot, cleared of oats by the first of August, putting in barley, however, in place of millet, as this is not injured by the early frosts. Barley may also be sown on the lot which was cropped about the tenth of August, or if this grain has already occupied the land, we may substitute corn, using a stimulating fertilizer to give it a rapid growth. In this way, we shall have a succession of green food up to November, augmented also by the tops of the roots when thinned out or when harvested. The larger varieties of the sweet corn may be substituted for the flat, and is perhaps better relished, although not affording perhaps so large a yield.

The twenty square rods devoted to root culture must receive attention as early in the season as possible—certainly by the first of May. The ground having been deeply plowed or spaded, and thoroughly manured, should be made perfectly level. The large sugar beet and the mangold wurzel are the most valuable for the milch cow, and may be sown at the rate of about six pounds to the acre. During their growth, careful attention should be given to them by keeping them free from weeds, and the surface of the ground loose and fresh. A good yield would give an average of about six hundred and fifty bushels to the acre, which will be eighty bushels for the plot of twenty square rods, and allowing the cow one-third of a bushel per day for the eight months of dry food. The roots should be secured from frost by placing them in the cellar or in deep pits well protected. The hundred rods which is to be devoted to the winter feeding, must be put down to oats at the same time, and exactly in the same manner as the first ten rods for summer soiling. Cut these when in their most succulent condition, which will be probably from the fifth to the tenth of July. Cure them well, and house or stack them in a suitable manner. The land having been again suitably prepared, the preceding crop must be at once followed by Hungarian grass, a bushel and a half to the acre, which will be fit for cutting as soon as the head is formed, which will be in about six weeks from the time of sowing. Cure it as far as possible in the cock, which will render it more nutritious.

The one hundred square rods being again cleared and put in order during the autumn, sow winter rye at the rate of three bushels to the acre. This will be ready to cut in the spring, and will afford green food much earlier than in any other way for soiling. If there is a surplus of any of the green crops, convert it into hay for winter use.

From the two croppings of the one hundred square rods, treated in the above manner, a fair yield will be a ton and a quarter of oats cured as hay, with an equal amount of Hungarian grass. Thus we have two and one-half tons of fodder, which will be amply sufficient for one cow through the eight months in which she is not receiving the green crops, allowing her the amount of hay per day which we have stated as necessary in conjunction with the roots and grain, in the quantities before mentioned.

Of course, where the feeding commences in April, if the place be taken in that month, food must be bought by the owner to last until the summer soiling in July. In the succeeding year, however, the crop of winter rye will come in early, to be used in conjunction with the dried fodder of the previous summer.

COW STABLED IN THE TOWN.

Again, there are cases where a single cow may be kept with profit and advantage, and that, too, in perfect health, without the agency of land, in the immediate suburbs of a town or city, or even within the very precincts of a city. It is requisite, for these conditions, that provision should be made to allow the animal to breathe fresh air, and to enjoy a certain amount of sunlight daily. Without these none should be kept. Exercise is not essential to the well-being of the milch cow; she is an animal of repose, and if she is offered every effort to ruminate, will be perfectly contented, and will do her duty. Attention to the best possible condition of the skin, as regards cleanliness, is very important when so closely housed.

The food which, under these circumstances, must be purchased, can be obtained with much economy, on account of the propinquity to the places of sale; and although we do not advocate the use of brewers' grain, or of any other cheap articles which are too often substituted for the natural food of the cow, viz., grass, green or dry—a small quantity, especially when supplemented by the vegetable refuse from the house table, may be advantageously employed conjointly with good hay.

Finally, it may be said that no animal better repays care and attention, and can with more truth be called the poor man's friend, than the cow.

FACTS REFUTE PREJUDICE.
BY D. B. CHAPMAN, NEW LONDON, CT.

When I was a boy it was the prevailing opinion in the section of country where I was raised, that it was better that a cow should be rather thin in flesh at the time of calving than otherwise. There was but very little grain fed in winter, to any stock in that section, except to working oxen. Cows in milk were fed hay, while dry cows, and young stock, were fed on straw or corn stalks. The result was that at the time of calving, cows were generally thin enough to conform to the popular idea of a proper condition. Cows giving a large yield of milk were scarce enough in those days, and it was very seldom that you would meet one that would yield ten quarts of milk per day (beer measure), during the flush of feed. My faith in the theory, that a cow should be thin in flesh at the time of calving, received a very severe shock, very soon after I became the owner of one, and experience and observation have only served to confirm my doubts of its correctness.

In the spring of 1848, I purchased my first cow. I came across her some twenty miles from home. She had just calved, and displayed a very large udder. Her owner warranted her to give twelve quarts of milk per day, and to be, in every respect, a good family cow. The cow suited my fancy in every particular, save one, she was too fat. But having nine points in her favor, I did not feel disposed to forego her purchase for the want of the tenth. When I drove her home, the adverse criticism on her was immense, solely on account of her condition. Said an old farmer to me: "That is a fancy cow, just suited for some rich man, who can afford to indulge his fancy, and expend for her keeping, twice as much as the value of her milk. You will find that you have got to keep her in just the condition that she is now in, or you will get no milk. If you do not keep her in this condition, you will find she will shrink in milk, before she shrinks in flesh, and she won't give half as much, on the same keeping, as she would if she was no fatter than my cows."

I must own, that after listening to this and that criticism in the same strain, I felt a little sick of my bargain, and would have willingly sold her at a discount, but no purchaser appearing, I concluded to make the best of a bad bargain.

My purchase was made April second. Twelve hundred pounds of hay furnished her with feed until the eighteenth of May. I then hired a pasture, for fifteen dollars, where I kept her until November, when I sold her.

KEEPING ONE COW.   111

I found that, although the cow lost flesh under my keeping, and a good deal of it too, she gave quite as much milk as she was recommended to give, and at the time she was sold, her account stood as follows, no account having been made of the milk used in the family, then consisting of three persons:

CR.

By sale of Milk, at 6 cents per quart		$74 20
do.	Calf	5 00
do.	Cow, November 1	18 00

$97 20

DR.

To purchase, April 2d		$35 00
do.	Hay	12 00
do.	Service	0 50
do	Pasture	15 00

$62 50

Net Profit...$34 70

I was so well pleased with this result, notwithstanding the unfavorable circumstance of having started with a fat cow, that the next spring I repurchased her at the same price paid the spring previous. But instead of a fat cow then, she was thin enough to afford a good study of animal anatomy. She had had no other feed than corn stalks, for the two months that she had been dry, and was as much thinner than when I sold her; as she was at that time thinner than when I first bought her. In fact, she had been subjected to a gradual system of depletion for a year.

I sold her on the first of October, following, when her account stood as follows, no account having been made of the milk used in the family, numbering three persons, as before:

DR.

To purchase	$35 00
Hay	12 00
Service	0 50
Meal	6 00
Pasture, the same as the previous year	15 00

$68 50

CR.

By sale of Milk, at 6 cents per quart		$51 30
do.	Calf, two weeks old	3 00
do.	Cow, October 1	12 00

$66 30

Loss...$2 20

This difference in profit was occasioned solely by the difference of the yield of her milk in the two seasons. The yield for the second season averaged full three quarts per day less than the first, and, at the same time, the quality of the milk was deteriorated in the same proportion as the quantity.

This was my first lesson, acquired by experience. At the same time, I learned another by observation. The two combined added materially to my stock of knowledge.

A neighbor of mine, a German, in the month of January, 1849, purchased a heifer, three years of age the coming spring. She had been kept poor from the time she was weaned. At two years of age she had dropped her first calf, and through her first season of milk had given but little promise as a milker. She had just been dried when he purchased her, and he, without any previous knowledge of the care of cows, commenced feeding her according to his instincts. He fed her six quarts of meal per day, in addition to all the hay she would eat. This system of feeding continued until about the twenty-fifth of March, when she calved. At the time of calving she was in better condition than much of the beef sold in our markets.

About the same time that his cow calved I repurchased mine. The feed of the two, thereafter, was very nearly alike, except that his cow had a feed of six quarts of meal per day, while mine had only two. His fat cow doubled on the quantity of milk that she had given the year before, when she came in poor, while my poor cow, with extra feed, fell short more than a third of her yield of the year before, when she came in, in good condition.

At that time I do not remember to have ever seen a work on chemistry, and knew nothing of its application; but the knowledge acquired, led to the formation of a theory in my mind, on which I have since acted, and which, I believe, has a scientific basis, to wit: "The fat laid on the body of an in-calf cow, is a store from which nature draws a large portion of the material which increases and enriches the subsequent flow of milk—a store from which she, by legitimate processes, produces oleo-stearine in the shape of butter."

Acting upon this theory, I have endeavored to apportion to my cows a uniform daily ration, occasionally varying the material, which, although it may not sustain the cow in full flesh during the greatest flow of milk, seems to renew it during the period of the lesser flow, and render them in good condition at the time of calving. This system of uniform feeding, to my mind, pays better than it does to feed heavily while in milk, and then l'ghtly when dry, because it furnishes a large resource of fat, on which to draw at a time when to consume sufficient food to sustain the entire flow of milk capable of being produced, might imperil health; and I feel quite sure that a certain richness is thereby imparted to the milk, that no amount of feeding will draw from a poor cow. In the autumn of 1877 I purchased a grade heifer reputed to be seven-eighths Jersey and one-eighth Ayrshire. She had dropped her first calf the spring previous, when only two years old. She was then represented as yielding three quarts of milk per day, and due to calve April the sixth. To account for the small yield of milk, her owner said she had been kept on poor pasture and milked by careless boys, who had not been particular to milk her clean.

That she had been kept on poor pasture her appearance abundantly confirmed. She came into my possession during the root harvest, in November. I commenced by feeding to her three bushels of rutabaga tops, or of beet tops, three pounds of corn meal, together with all the dry hay she would eat each day.

ONE YEAR'S EXPENSES AND RETURNS.

The cost of keeping the cow from November first, 1877, to June first, 1878, was as follows:

150 pounds of Indian Meal, at $1 40		$ 2 10
380 "	Ship Stuff, at $1 35	5 13
140 "	Oil Meal, at $1 30	1 82
4140 "	Roots, at $8 00 per ton	16 56
3392 "	Hay, at $20	33 92
1 peck Salt		0 25
		$59 73

The cost from June first to November first, 1878, was as follows:

1530 pounds of Hay, at $20		$15 30
225 "	Oil meal, at $1 30	2 92
470 "	Bran, at $1 35	6 35
Salt		0 25
Service		2 00
		$26 82

Making a total cost of $86 60

for the year, counting nothing for the garden truck consumed during the summer and autumn. This, with the exception of the corn stalks, would have been consigned to the compost heap, had she not eaten it, so that its only value to me was its value for compost. But allowing that for the purpose of feed it was equal in value to its equivalent in hay, and that my winter ration of hay had been continued through the year, her total cost of keeping would have been, in round numbers, one hundred and four dollars.

In the roots fed to her during the winter, were included the waste and parings of vegetables used in a family of ten persons, which was sometimes no inconsiderable item. These were always thrown into the feed basket, and just enough fresh roots sliced to make the required weight. After the roots stored in the cellar were exhausted no account was made of this item. I make this statement simply to show that every item of feed was entered at its full value, into the cost of the keeping.

Now for the other side. Although the cow was quite thin when I bought her, yet under this system of care and feeding, she was estimated to have gained two hundred pounds in weight by the time she calved, on the fifteenth of April, 1878, and of this weight she had not lost more than seventy-five pounds at the end of the year, November first. When I bought her she was represented as yielding three quarts of milk per day. Her yield of milk weighed on the first day exactly five and three-quarter pounds. At the end of three weeks, it had increased to eleven pounds per day, and continued at this figure with scarcely any interruption until the first of February. It then rapidly fell off, until by the twenty-fifth of that month, she yielded only seven pounds per day. I then commenced milking her once a day, and the milking on the fourth day after weighed only four and a half pounds. I continued milking her until the fifteenth of March, when I stopped, the weight of the last milking being only one and three-quarter pounds. On the tenth of April she calved. I let her calf suckle her until it was four weeks old, when it was sold for veal. On the seventh of May her yield of milk was twenty-two pounds. It averaged about that figure until she got a full feed of pea vines in June, when it ran up as high as twenty-seven pounds. In July it fell off some, and continued to run from twenty to twenty-three pounds until the middle of August. It then gradually diminished to the first of November, at which time she was yielding thirteen pounds of milk per day. I find, by referring to my diary, that her total yield of milk from the time I purchased her until she calved, was one thousand and sixty-seven pounds, equal to four hundred and eighty-four quarts, reckoning thirty-four ounces to the quart. Milk was then selling, in this vicinity, at six cents per quart, making a value of twenty-six dollars and four cents.

From the time she calved until the first of November, her total yield of milk was three thousand seven hundred and seventy-seven pounds, equal to one thousand seven hundred and seventy-seven quarts, at five cents, eighty-eight dollars and eighty-five cents; sale of calf, six dollars and fifty-cents; making a net profit of seventeen dollars and thirty-nine cents, to say nothing of the growth of the cow, or the value of her manure, which was an ample compensation for the care of keeping.

Had I estimated the value of her milk at the retail price, I should add one cent per quart for summer, and two cents per quart for winter. The next year this same cow, with the increase of the equivalent of one and a half pounds of meal per day, to allow for her increased growth, and a slight deviation in the matter of feed during the summer, whereby she obtained more green food, of which I shall speak hereafter, increased her profit almost forty per cent.

GARGET.

Of one thing I am very careful, and that is, not to allow the inflowing milk, previous to calving, to harden in the udder, and in all my long experience, in owning cows, I have never had a case of garget. When I was a boy about twelve years of age, my father purchased a very large milker for those days. I noticed that the right hind quarter of her udder was much smaller than the other, and yielded a correspondingly less quantity of milk. After she had been dried off, and the time approached for her to calve, I observed that this same quarter of her udder became very much more distended than the others. Her whole udder was very much distended, but this quarter excessively so. As her period of calving was delayed, and her udder became more inflamed, producing, evidently, great pain to the cow, I asked the privilege of milking her, and was denied. At the same time I was given to understand that it was the worst possible thing that could be done for the cow; that it was necessary that her udder should become thus distended, in order to give it the capacity to contain the flow of milk after calving; that should she be milked before calving, the yield after calving would be very much lessened, etc. By the time she calved, her udder was one indurated mass, and that particular quarter of it so much inflamed that she could not bear to have the calf touch it. In the course of time, however, by copious applications of cold water, and various liniments, the inflammation was reduced, but that particular section of the udder, which had been sufficiently distended to hold her whole yield, was shrunken to its old dimensions, and was no larger than when I first saw her. When the time approached for her to drop her next calf, I took the responsibility of clandestinely milking her, so that when she calved there was no inflamed udder, there was no fussing with liniments. Its four quarters were now evenly developed; the only difference was the former shrunken quarter was larger, if anything, than the others, and, throughout the season, the yield of milk, from the same keeping, was essentially increased over the yield of the previous year. I never disclosed the secret, however, until I was grown up. But I acquired a very useful lesson which I applied in my practice long before the theory that it was best to milk a cow previous to calving was generally adopted by owners around me.

TETHERING.

A professional friend of mine is the owner of three horses and two imported cows, all of which are kept in very high condition. He informs me that for several years, with the exception of one year, two and one half acres of land have furnished all the hay consumed by the five animals, together with pasturage for one cow; the other cow being dry during the summer, is pastured in the country. His land is naturally good grass land, being moist, well drained, and perfectly smooth. The apparatus for tethering his cow, when at pasture, consists of a pole or joist, the short end of which is weighted, swiveled on an iron upright, standing, when in position, about four feet above the ground, giving the apparatus the appearance of a model of an old-fashioned well sweep. The halter being attached to the upper end, is always above her back while feeding. This arrangement allows the cow the range of a circuit thirty feet in diameter. The upright is removed to the arc of the circle at morning and noon. In this manner she traverses the length of the lot, four hundred feet, in fourteen days, when she is brought back to the starting point, to repeat the journey again. In this manner, twelve thousand feet of land is made to furnish pasturage for one cow during the entire summer, and besides this, she has no feed whatever. The cow is always in good condition, and the ground never appears very closely cropped, and I have no doubt that were she restricted to one quarter of an acre, or ten thousand eight hundred and ninety feet, she would still be better fed than most cows that are at pasture. The droppings of the cow are daily removed from this range, so that she always has a clean feeding ground. All the manure made by the five animals is annually returned to this lot, and, in addition, the owner informs me, once in three years he gives it a dressing of a ton of ground bone.

PEARL MILLET.

After reading of Mr. Peter Henderson's experiment with Pearl Millet, as described in the "American Agriculturist," I determined to make a trial with it myself. Accordingly, last year, I sowed an area of eighteen square rods with it, in drills, fourteen inches apart; six rods were set apart to be cut and dried for fodder. The product of the other twelve rods was fed green. On the twentieth of June, a month after sowing, the growth measured about three feet in hight. On this date we commenced cutting it, and feeding to the cow all she would eat. She ate it with a greater apparent relish than any other green feed that had been given her. The cutting was finished on the twenty-fifth of July, on which day the last cutting measured about four feet in hight. The second cutting was commenced on the twenty-seventh of July, and finished on the twenty-second of August, the growth averaging nearly three and a half feet. The third cutting was commenced on the twenty-third and finished on the thirty-first of August. The growth was about two feet at the beginning of the cutting, but not more than ten inches at the finish. The fourth and last cutting was commenced on the sixteenth, and finished on the twenty-first of September, after which the ground appeared exhausted, and no further growth was made. The twelve rods cut and fed green yielded feed sufficient for seventy-five days, aside from her usual ration of bran or oil meal, while the product from the six rods, cut and fed dry, only two cuttings being made, was sufficient to feed her for thirty-four days, making a total feed for one hundred and nine days, from eighteen rods of ground; at which rate it would require sixty and one-quarter rods of ground to furnish forage for a year.

AN EXCELLENT COMPOST.

The only stable manure I use on my crops is that made by my cow. All my other fertilizers are artificially produced. In the course of the year, in prosecuting my regular business, I render some two hundred thousand pounds of tallow. This is all done by boiling it with sulphuric acid. The acid attacks and decomposes the animal tissue, leaving the rendered tallow floating on its surface. A part of the dissolved animal tissue, together with the bones that are sometimes smuggled in with the rough fat, settles to the bottom of the tanks, and a part remains dissolved in the acid. This spent acid, together with the deposit in the bottom of the tanks, is the source of all my nitrogen, except what may be in the manure from the cow, as well as a portion of my phosphorous. I have occasion to use considerable of the potash of commerce in some of my manufactures. For my land, I make of this a saturated solution, and then dry it, by stirring into it a mixture of equal parts of ground plaster and sifted coal ashes. This, in a few days, becomes sulphate of potash, lime, and coal ashes, at least I judge that it does, for it loses all its causticity.

In preparing my fertilizers, I mix the product of my tanks with loam, near the place to be planted; this, in the spring, is dug over and mixed with the manure from the stable. The effect of this mixing is to make the manure very fine in a very short time. After plowing, this compost is spread upon the land, and harrowed in. I then follow with ground bone, which costs me, delivered at my place, bolted, twenty-five dollars per ton, at the rate of twelve hundred pounds to the acre, and with the potash mixture, at the rate of two hundred and forty pounds to the acre, which is also harrowed in. In distributing the potash, I distribute more of it where I intend to plant peas or potatoes, and less where I intend to plant corn, squashes, and turnips. In distributing the bone, I reverse this. It is on a light, sandy loam, fertilized in this manner, with an excess of nitrogen, no doubt, that I expect, the coming summer, to raise enough feed for a cow on less than half an acre of ground. The land on which my experiment was tried last year was a turned sod that had had no manure of any kind for more than ten years. This year it will be tried on land that was manured as above last year.

A WOMAN'S SUCCESS AND EXPERIENCE.

BY MRS. MARY L. TAYLOR, NORTH VERNON, INDIANA.

My success in keeping the family cow is mainly due to the superior sense of that animal in coming into being in a latitude where a cow can live with as little care and protection, and where the face of unplowed and unharrowed nature furnishes as much food for her as any other; latitude thirty-nine.

My cow is a scrub—cost twenty dollars; had her calf on the fourteenth of February, 1879, and we complimented the saint on whose day she came by calling her Valentine.

HOW WE MANAGED THE CALF.

I put the calf in a pen made in the fence corner and covered with a few old boards, and let the cow in to her every night—first taking from the cow what milk we needed for our family of four persons. I left her with the calf all night, and in the morning milked what the calf had left for me. This was not much after the first two weeks, and after two more weeks I only wasted my time at milking in the morning. I parted with the calf at three months old for eight dollars, and laid this sum by as my capital to draw against for the cow's winter keeping.

My farm is half an acre in extent, and all of it, except the space occupied by the cottage and a small garden, is lawn, and is well set in Blue-grass, with a sprinkling of Orchard-grass.

SUMMER MANAGEMENT.

I sold my lawn mower and put a short rope around my cow's horns. To this I fastened the chain of an old chain-pump. The pump had served its day, and was now laid aside. This old pump-chain was about sixteen feet long, and through the end of it I stuck an old iron garden stake into the ground, and staked my cow out on the lawn. In the chain I put rings one yard apart, and by running my garden stake through a ring nearer or farther from the rope around the cow's horns, I could give her a larger or smaller circle to graze on, and so let her eat very near to evergreens and other shrubbery without danger of having them injured. She pulled up the stake several times at first, but the remedy for this came of itself. In my desire to make her very secure, I had tied the rope around her horns too tightly and made her head sore. She ceased pulling, and though her head soon got well, she has never since pulled up the stake; so that my mistake in fastening the rope, though it caused me self-reproaches at the time, really proved a blessing in the end, for had she formed the habit of pulling the stake up, I should have been forced to discontinue staking her out for fear of her destroying the shrubbery. My cow seems to have a spite at shrubbery proportioned to its beauty, and this spite seems intensified against such plants as she cannot eat. A young cedar, for instance, she will never pass without trying to demolish it with her horns. By means of the rings in my chain, I could stake her so that she could eat up to the edge of an evergreen without being able to touch it with her horns, and I found the horns the only part that the shrubbery had to fear, for she never yet has tried to destroy anything with her heels.

My lawn, under the care of this new one-cow lawn-mower, became the admiration and envy of the whole neighborhood. The chickens followed her and scattered her droppings, so that the lawn was always clean. I found it a great improvement on the old hand lawn-mower, and much less labor, for the staking out was far less trouble than running the mower. Besides, I sold the old machine for almost half the price I paid for the cow. But, strange as it seems to me now, I at first felt a little ashamed of my new mower, for I got in the practice of staking the cow on the front lawn at night, and moving her to the back lawn early in the morning.

She did her work so silently in the darkness that my neighbors wondered much that in so well-kept a lawn they never heard the click of the lawn-mower.

We have no storms in the summer in this latitude from which a cow needs any more protection than a tree affords. When it rained I milked her under the shelter of a beech.

In June, I rented a one-quarter acre lot for two dollars, and for one dollar hired it plowed and laid off in furrows a little over two feet apart. In these furrows I dropped corn, the grains two to four inches apart. I hired it plowed once with a shovel plow. This cost seventy-five cents. At the first frost, I had it cut and put up in small shocks. A woman that does washing for me, and occasionally chores about the house, did this at forty cents a day. She was several days at it, but during the time performed other work about the house. I think she spent about two solid days on it. This corn-fodder, with few large ears on it, but a great many nubbins, made my fodder and grain for the cow for the winter. Later in the fall, when the corn-stalks were thoroughly cured, I had them placed against poles set on crotches around the place where the cow was sheltered during the winter. The stalks were leaned against the poles from both sides, and made a sloping roof both ways, so as to shed snow and rain. From these poles I gave the cow an armful of this corn and fodder night and morning, and though the snow did sometimes lodge on them, and make my mittens cold, I could generally find a spot on one side or the other that was clear of snow. This work of putting up the fodder for winter use cost about two dollars.

My cow had been used to "slops" and meal, and did not take kindly to whole corn at first. I was advised to husk the corn, and get it ground; but by feeding her a few small or broken, or soft ears from my hand, she soon became eager for it, and has learned to grind it as well as the mill, and at less cost of going to and from, to say nothing of the toll. But even if she was not as good a corn crusher as the mill-stones, there would be no loss, for my fowls follow her faithfully, and pick up every broken grain that is dropped; so the miller's toll that I save keeps me in chickens and eggs. Now that the cow had come to eat whole corn, I was told that she would muss over the fodder, hunting for the nubbins, and waste the stalks; but by sprinkling a little brine on the stalks when she became dainty, I found I could make her eat them as closely as was desirable.

A WINTER SHELTER.

I had no stable. The cow stood out in all the storms until late in December. The hair grew very thick, almost like a buffalo robe, and she did not seem to mind the cold. There was an old chicken house on the place, standing on posts about five feet high. It was in a hollow, and was sheltered by evergreens on the north and west. As I pulled up her stake one night in a drizzle to let her go under the tree where I milked her, she started on the gallop for this house, and from that time it was her winter couch. There I milked and fed her. I tied the chain around one of the corner posts, so as to leave her the choice of the shelter of the building or of exposure to the storm at her discretion, and I must say that she often surprised me by seeming as fond as a child of standing out in the rain. Under this coop I fed her fodder; the stalks she left, littered down her bed, and I had more manure in the spring than I had ever had before. A boy spread it from a wheelbarrow at twenty-five cents a day. The spring before I paid fifty cents a load for the manure, and two dollars and fifty cents a day for the hauling.

ABOUT SALTING.

I never fed the cow any salt for health during the summer, but she kept healthy, and the butter came. In the fall, I began feeding her the house slops, night and morning, and when she did not eat them freely I put a little salt in. When I thought she was not eating her fodder up clean enough, I would sprinkle on a little brine with an old broom. I never fed salt for her good, but sometimes for mine. In the fall, when I wanted her to eat up weeds before they went to seed, I used occasionally to sprinkle with brine such spots as I wanted eaten off closely. I never could make my old lawn-mower cut off weeds any closer than grass, but this new lawn-mower would eat these weed patches to the collars of the roots.

My cow became used to this kind of life, makes me no trouble, has furnished the milk and butter for our family of four the whole year, and some butter to send to my friends, and a little to sell. I have fodder enough from my quarter acre to keep her until grass is abundant, and have one dollar and twenty cents of the price of my calf still on hand.

I might go on and tell you how I used to buy hay at a high price for wintering my cow, and quantities of bran, brewers' grains and corn-meal; how the hay always made her costive and hide-bound, and how she never ate it with half the relish which she does the corn fodder; how I found it an unladylike act to raise my foot and force the garden stake into the ground, and so contrived a smaller iron that I could more gracefully plant, and that no unruly cow ever could pull up; how with this new stake I can safely leave her on the lawn all night with the fullest confidence of finding her in the morning just where I left her; how when at first the cow got loose and wandered to the garden, I discovered that the taste of the butter was disagreeably affected by her eating certain herbs, and how it was very pleasantly flavored by others; how I am cultivating these herbs to make the sweetest and most golden butter; how—but dear me! for a one-cow story it is already too long,

FIG. 23.—THE JERSEY COW "ABBIE."

UNDERDRAINING AND CARE OF MANURE.
BY H. H. HALL, NEW ORLEANS, LA.

Let us locate one acre of land on the thirty-eighth degree of north latitude, midway across the continent, say near the City of St. Louis. While under the intensive system of cultivation which will be pursued, less land than one acre will ultimately be found sufficient to supply the wants of one cow, it would not be advisable to begin with a less quantity. That one acre is sufficient is opposed to the general opinion, as witness the assertion of Mr. Schull, of Little Falls, N. Y., that the land in pasturage and hay, requisite for the support of one cow, is three acres, and this accords with the estimate of Mr. Carrington for moderately good dairy farms in England. Colman says: Three acres are required for a cow in Berksire Co., Mass. Mr. Farrington, in the Report of the American Dairymen's Association says, four; while Mr. X. A. Willard thinks that in Herkimer Co., N. Y., one and a half to two acres will pasture one cow, and that in some exceptional cases one acre will suffice.

True it is that these estimates take into consideration grass and hay solely, and the treatment of the land is presumed to be that usually pursued, viz.: scant allowance of manure, absence of subsoil drainage, and consequently shallow cultivation.

But high manuring and deep cultivation are indispensable in view, viz.: the obtaining the greatest quantity of dairy food from the least land. And high cultivation, implying depth of soil, tilth, porosity and aeration is impossible without subsoil drainage; nor in its absence does manure produce its best effects. It is foreign to the purpose of this article to elucidate the action of tile draining upon crops and soil. The lasting and great benefit of the system is, to-day, a matter of such plain fact, that no intelligent agriculturist will question it.

Therefore we begin by selecting an acre of land which affords the best facilities for laying tile-drainage pipes. An easy slope with a good, open outlet into ditch, run, or gulch, is all that is required. The advantages of a sunny exposure are so obvious that, if possible, we should choose land which trends to the south and east. The tile-draining of one acre will necessitate an outlay of about twenty-five dollars; but this expenditure is indispensable to the obtaining of the best results.

THE DUNG HEAP.

Truly did the German agriculturist, Schwerz, in seeing the fertile streamlets oozing and trickling away from the exposed manure piles of his opinionated countrymen, denonimate the dung heap the "Fountainhead of Benediction." This, like other blessings, may but too readily be perverted in its uses.

Impressed with the necessity of husbanding every part and portion of this substratum of good agriculture, we choose between two distinct methods of saving and utilizing the fluid and solid *dejecta*, viz.: the dry and wet. In the former the *dejecta* are commingled with such absorbents as dry earth, leaves, straw, sawdust, etc.; in the latter, they are received in a tank where they are mixed with sufficient water to stay loss by too rapid fermentation.

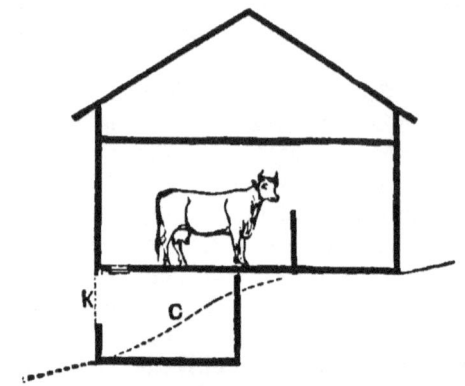

Fig. 24.—A COW STABLE WITH MANURE CELLAR.

The application of the manure under either method is respectively in its dry or in its liquid condition.

If the dry or absorbent method be adopted, it will be found advantageous to locate the stable on a little declivity, so as to secure a manure cellar with the least excavation.

Thus, in fig. 24, *C* represents a manure cellar under the cow, with a door at *K* for removal of manure. The floor and walls, to a hight of two feet, of this cellar should be cemented. The floor, on which the cow stands, should be of two-inch oak plank, with a gutter behind, and a trap to empty the contents of the gutter into the cellar. On level tracts of ground the Flemish stable, as used in parts of the Brabant, and as described in the following plan fig. 25, by Felix Villeroy (Manuel de l'Eleveur de Bètes, à Comes, 6 Ed., p. 63), could be advantageously used for one cow. In figure 25, *A* is the place where the cow stands; *B*, Passage for distributing food, etc.; *C*, Depression where the manure is allowed to accumulate behind the cow; *D*, Cellar for roots; *E*, Hay loft.

In this plan the floor A and C would require to be finished in brick and cement, or concrete.

The warmth of the stable might, at times, develop a too rapid fermentation of the manure. This would be checked by working the pile and by forking it over.

But to secure perfect cleanliness, purity of air, and freedom of the hay stored above from the odors of fermentation going on in the

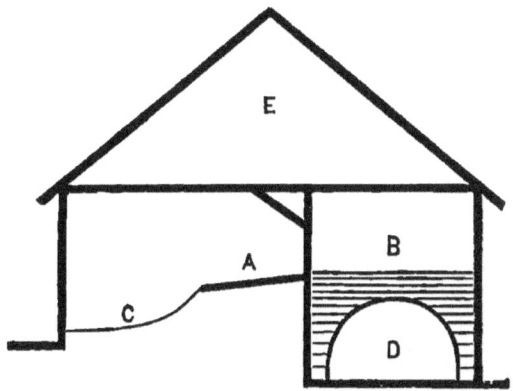

Fig. 25.—SECTIONAL VIEW OF STABLE.

dung heap, the manure would be better placed outside of the stable walls, as suggested in figure 26 (see next page).

The bottom of the manure bin is only twenty-four inches below the surface, as on level ground the labor of raising the manure from a deep cellar would be disproportionate to the advantages of the depth. The floor of the stall should be laid in brick and cement, or in concrete, as should be the floor and lower walls of the manure bin. The floor of the stall should be kept covered with dry earth, leaves, sawdust, or spent tan-bark; and the bottom of the bin should be covered to the depth of several inches, with similar absorbents. In the absence of these to-be-preferred materials, weeds, straw, or other dry vegetable refuse, may be used. With the gutter sufficiently inclined, the excessive urine will of itself flow readily to the bin; the solid matter should be removed twice daily, just before the cow is milked. The gutter should be washed down with a pail of water daily, and sprinkled with gypsum (sulphate of lime). The manure pile, as it increases, should be constantly commingled with fresh absorbents. This is most readily and economically done by baiting a pig with a handful of maize cast on the manure in the bin. The lusty porker will go to the bottom of the pile, it need be, for each grain, and by his energetic rooting and trampling, will daily incorporate the materials in the most thorough manner.

On page 260 of Boussingault's Rural Economy (Law's translation) are some very urgent warnings against the frequent turning of dung heaps. His objection, Mr. Law thinks, should be limited to more than three turnings of the dung. But this objection and limitation apply to horse manure, the more active fermentation of which rapidly develops the highly volatile salt known as carbonate of ammonia. There can hardly be too thorough a working

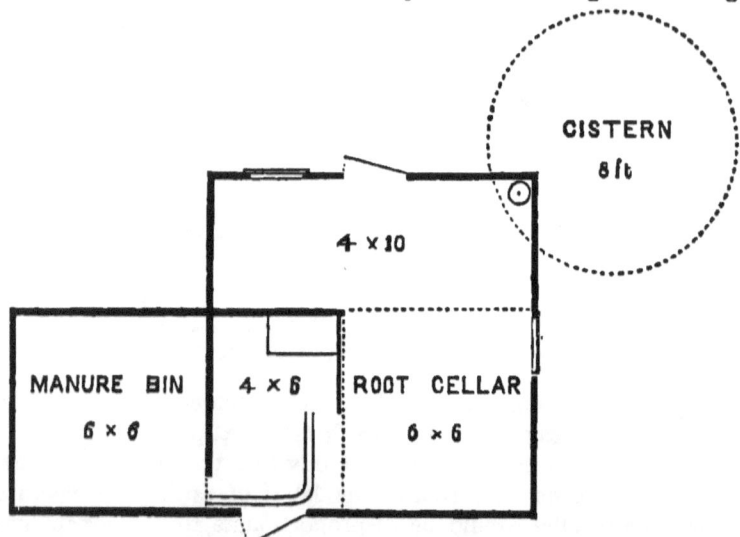

Fig. 26.—PLAN OF STABLE WITH CISTERN AND MANURE BIN.

together of cow-manure, with its organic absorbents, particularly when the working is accompanied by the compacting tread of animals.

The pile should be watched, and the slightest perception of the pungent ammoniacal odor should be the signal for more absorbents, bearing in mind that all organic matter thus composted becomes a valuable fertilizer, and remembering that nothing should be left undone to increase to the greatest extent possible the source of your anticipated blessings.

The manure bin should, of course, be so covered as to exclude rain and sunshine.

If the liquid or dilute method be employed, in place of the manure bin in the plan, it will be necessary to construct an underground cemented tank or cistern, say of a depth of eight feet and diameter of six to seven feet at the bottom. This tank must be provided with a pump for raising the fluid, the tube of which should terminate in a strainer at about twelve inches from the bottom of the tank. An opening should be left in the top of the cistern for inspection, and for the insertion of a proper implement to stir the sediment. The pump should rise sufficiently high to permit the pumping of the fluid directly into a tank on wheels used for the distribution thereof in the fields. A condemned watering cart, which could probably be purchased cheaply, would be an excellent instrument for this distribution. Sulphate of iron, green vitriol, should be freely used to change the carbonate of ammonia into the sulphate, thereby obtaining a fixed, instead of a highly volatile salt.

KEEPING A COW IN A VILLAGE STABLE.

BY ORANGE JUDD, FLUSHING, L. I.

A business man of New York, living in one of the neighboring villages, being troubled to get good milk for young children in his family, took our advice the latter part of the winter and, so to speak, went into the dairy business on his own account. The result will be instructive to tens of thousands of families in cities and villages. He has no pasture grounds, the only convenience being a roomy stall in a carriage barn, with opportunity for the cow to sun herself and take limited exercise in a small area, say fifteen by twenty feet, at the side of the barn, and this was seldom used. The stall is kept clean and neat, with fresh straw litter, and the cow has remained in excellent health and vigor. Chewing her cud and manufacturing milk seem to give all the exercise needed. Her feed has been bale hay, cut in a small hay-cutter, and mixed wet with corn-meal, bran, and shorts, with some uncooked potato parings, cabbage leaves, left over rice, oatmeal, etc., from the kitchen.

A laborer is paid one dollar a week to milk and feed and brush her night and morning, and take care of the stable, and he is allowed any excess of milk she gives over twelve quarts a day. He prepares a mess for her noon feed, which is given by one of the boys at school when he comes home to lunch. The cow is a grade, probably three-fourths Jersey and one-fourth common blood. Her milk is rich, yields abundant cream, and, as the owner's family say, "Is worth fully double any milk we ever got from the best milk dealers." One neighboring family gladly takes six quarts a day at seven cents a quart, and would willingly pay much more if it were asked, and other families would be happy to get some of it at ten cents a quart; but six quarts are kept for home use, and it is valued far above seven cents a quart, and worth more than that amount in the saving of butter in cooking, making puddings, etc. So it is a very low estimate to call the whole milk worth seven cents a quart. No one could deprive our business friend or his family of their good, home produced milk, if it cost ten or twelve cents a quart. An accurate account is kept of the feed; the man in charge orders at the feed store anything he desires for the cow, and it is all down on a "pass-book." Here are the figures for one hundred days past:

THE COW'S DEBIT AND CREDIT FOR ONE HUNDRED DAYS.

Dr.

850 lbs. bale Hay, at $22 per ton	$9 35
1,000 lbs. Corn Meal, at $1.35 per 100 lbs	13 50
400 lbs. Bran, at $1.30 per 100 lbs	5 20
200 lbs. Fine Feed, "Shorts," at $1.55 per 100 lbs	3 10
20 bundles of bedding Straw, at 10c	2 00
Paid man for care and milking, $1 per week	14 30
Total expenses for 100 days	$47 45

Cr.

1,200 Quarts of best milk (12 quarts per day) at 7c	$84 00
Money profit in 100 days	$36 55

Or, to put it in another way, the six hundred quarts sold actually brought in forty-two dollars cash, and the entire six hundred quarts used at home cost five dollars and forty-five cents. The cow cost, say, sixty-five dollars. The entire care, which was not paid in the surplus of milk above twelve quarts per day, is charged in the expenses above. The manure produced, if sold, would more than meet interest on the cost of cow, and any depreciation in value by increasing age. Allow the above average to be kept up only two hundred days in a year, and at the end of that time suppose the cow is sold for half price (thirty-two dollars and fifty cents), and a fresh one substituted, there would still be a gain of forty dollars and sixty cents for two hundred days, or for a year a profit of seventy-four dollars and ten cents.

With good feed the sixty-five dollar cow will keep up a full supply of milk at least twenty-six weeks, and then be worth forty dollars for continued milking and breeding. Sell her then and buy another fresh cow for sixty-five dollars—a loss of fifty dollars a year. The above liberal allowance of forty-seven dollars and forty-five cents for feed and care one hundred days, amounts to one hundred and seventy-three dollars and nineteen cents a year. Adding the loss of fifty dollars for purchasing two fresh cows, makes the total annual expense two hundred and twenty-three dollars and nineteen cents. This would make the supply of milk, twelve quarts a day (four thousand three hundred and eighty quarts), cost about five cents a quart, or not quite fifty-one cents for ten quarts. This is not an exaggerated estimate for a sixty-five dollar cow, renewed every twenty-six weeks. The feed and care may be very much less than the above forty-seven dollars and forty-five cents per hundred days, by saving all waste foods suitable for a cow, and by securing pasturage seven or eight months, and especially when a cow can be cared for by members of the family, thus saving fifty-two dollars a year. Taking the country as a whole, probably fifty dollars will ordinarily buy a cow that will, on fair feed, average ten to twelve quarts per day for the first six months after calving.

PORTRAITS OF FAMOUS DAIRY COWS.

I.—Jersey Cow "Eurotas," 2454 (*Frontispiece*), owned by A. B. Darling, Ramsey's, N. J. She yielded during one week in June, 1879, twenty-two pounds six ounces of butter.

II.—Ayrshire cow "Old Creamer" (page 23), owned by S. D. Hungerford, Adams, N. Y. Weight one thousand and eighty pounds. She has yielded one hundred and two-third pounds a day for three days, and ninety-four pounds a day for the month.

III.—Jersey cow "Rosalee," 1215 (page 34), owned by S. G. Livermore, Cedar Rapids, Iowa. She has given twenty quarts of milk a day. In ten days in June, 1874, she made twenty-five pounds three ounces of butter.

IV.—Guernsey cow and heifer (page 51), owned by Mr. Rendle, of Catel Parish, Island of Guernsey.

V.—Swiss cow "Geneva" (page 67), imported by D. G. Aldrich, of Worcester, Mass. She gave from November first, 1877, to December thirty-first, 1878, ten thousand nine hundred and five pounds of milk, which yielded five hundred and seventy-three pounds of butter.

VI.—Dutch (Holstein) cow "Crown Princess" (page 85), imported by Gerrit S. Miller, of Peterboro', N. Y. She has yielded thirty-four quarts of milk a day, and averaged twenty-three quarts a day for six months.

VII.—Shorthorn dairy cow "Cold Cream 4th" (page 101), owned by H. M. Queen Victoria. She is kept at the Shaw Farm, Windsor Home Park.

VIII.—Jersey cow "Abbie" (page 123), owned by Mr. Harvey Newton, of Southville, Mass. She yielded from April, 1876, to March, 1877, ten thousand seven hundred pounds of milk, from which four hundred and eighty six pounds of butter were made.

www.ingramcontent.com/pod-product-compliance
Lightning Source LLC
Chambersburg PA
CBHW022136160426
43197CB00009B/1312